CW00922387

Mothers in Israel

METHODIST BEGINNINGS
THROUGH THE EYES OF WOMEN

Donna L. Fowler-Marchant

Mothers in Israel: Methodist Beginnings Through the Eyes of Women

The General Board of Higher Education and Ministry leads and serves The United Methodist Church in the recruitment, preparation, nurture, education, and support of Christian leaders—lay and clergy—for the work of making disciples of Jesus Christ for the transformation of the world. Its vision is that a new generation of Christian leaders will commit boldly to Jesus Christ and be characterized by intellectual excellence, moral integrity, spiritual courage, and holiness of heart and life. The General Board of Higher Education and Ministry of The United Methodist Church serves as an advocate for the intellectual life of the church. The Board's mission embodies the Wesleyan tradition of commitment to the education of laypersons and ordained persons by providing access to higher education for all persons.

Wesley's Foundery Books is named for the abandoned foundery that early followers of John Wesley transformed, which later became the cradle of London's Methodist movement.

Mothers in Israel: Methodist Beginnings Through the Eyes of Women

Copyright 2021 by Wesley's Foundery Books

Wesley's Foundery Books is an imprint of the General Board of Higher Education and Ministry, The United Methodist Church. All rights reserved.

No part of this book may be reproduced in any form whatsoever, print or electronic, without written permission, except in the case of brief quotations embodied in critical articles or reviews. For information regarding rights and permissions, contact the Publisher, General Board of Higher Education and Ministry, PO Box 340007, Nashville, TN 37203-0007; phone 615-340-7393; fax 615-340-7048. Visit our website at www.gbhem.org.

All web addresses were correct and operational at the time of publication.

ISBN 978-1-945935-82-4

GBHEM Publishing is an affiliate member of the Association of University Presses.

Manufactured in the United States of America

HIGHER EDUCATION & MINISTRY
General Board of Higher Education and Ministry
THE UNITED METHODIST CHURCH

To the memory of my mother, Marie Fowler, who prayerfully educated me in the things of God. I am grateful for all the faithful women who have been mothers in Israel to me through the years. Last but not least, I give thanks for my husband, Scott Marchant, whose tolerance for a life dominated by multiple stacks of books and constant conversations about Methodism is nearly endless. His price is above rubies.

Contents

Introduction

The story of Methodism, like any story, is told from a particular slant, depending on the storyteller. John Wesley himself wanted to be the primary historian of the movement, defining and defending Methodism against the polemic and propaganda of its detractors. Not surprisingly in the process of doing so, he highlighted some aspects of the revival while downplaying and recasting others. Methodism came under attack for its supposed politically seditious nature, for the threat of divisiveness it posed within the Established Church, for alleged sexual license, and for its irregular practices of discipline and worship.[1]

Wesley could not have been surprised that Methodism provoked intense reactions. Despite his repeated protestations that it was a renewal society within the Church of England designed to spread scriptural holiness, many of the practical steps he took in his zeal to proclaim the gospel to as many people as possible looked more like the actions of the leader of yet another dissenting church group than of a high church Anglican priest and Fellow of Lincoln College.[2] When he "submitted to be more vile," following George Whitefield into the strange, new world of field preaching, even across parish boundaries; when he allowed, encouraged, and trained laymen to turn itinerant preacher; and when he cautiously then enthusiastically promoted the leadership of certain women not only over their own sex but over mixed groups, comparisons to Quakers and Baptists abounded, along with the dreaded epithet of "enthusiasm."[3]

"Of the making of books there is no end," says Qoheleth in Ecclesiastes 12, and much ink has been spilled in the endeavor to shed more light on the story of early Methodism; but curiously, the voices of women have been, if not unheard, at least misheard and under-heard. Even today, "current cataloging systems usually list the male editor as the author of the woman's writings; for example, Henry Moore is called the author of Mary Fletcher's journal."[4] The deep insights and reflections contained in women's diaries and journals were often suppressed, repackaged, and edited by men to make them more acceptable, and women's writings are largely unavailable today.[5] While a few scholars have painstakingly researched and shared the stories of some of these women, sadly, the average person who identifies with one of the branches of the Wesleyan family often knows little more than the name of Susanna Wesley and perhaps the name of one or two other early Methodist women and next to nothing of their immense contributions to Methodist witness and ministry.

Our forebears in the nineteenth century pored over the journals of Frances Mortimer Pawson, Hester Ann Roe Rogers, and Mary Bosanquet Fletcher, finding inspiration and deriving strength from their theological writings and biographies. Methodists of today likewise need to be aware of the debt we owe to them and women like them whose hearts were warmed and whose lives were changed by the experience of grace encountered in Methodist preaching houses and class meetings. Contemporary congregations who are shocked when a female pastor is appointed are frequently unaware that women in Methodist leadership is *not* a recent development nor an aberration in Wesleyan Methodism; they are woefully ignorant that women have functioned in leadership roles, both seen and unseen, in its witness and mission from the very beginning.

Mothers in Israel

Methodist women who displayed not only leadership but exemplary courage and devotion were sometimes called by an honorific that hearkens back to another exceptional woman in a traditionally male position of authority, Deborah the Old Testament judge. Like her, they were called "Mothers in Israel." This designation encompassed many aspects of what it is to be a mother, especially as provider, nurturer, protector, and healer, linking the spiritual and domestic spheres in which they operated.

Wesley used the language of home and family to represent his ideal vision for a community of believers, so all men were called "Brother" and all women "Sister." To be a "Mother in Israel" was rarer and therefore more distinguished.[6] Mary Bosanquet Fletcher and Sarah Crosby were among the early Methodist women honored with this title because of their faithful leadership, their holy boldness, and their great piety.

What compelled these strong, intelligent, pious women to stand fast in the face of obstacles? How did their faith give them a firm foundation on which to stand? How were they alike, and how were they different? And what were the reactions and roles of the significant men in their lives in either encouraging or impeding them in their ministries? Exploring their stories reveals a legacy of important shared spiritual qualities. Brought up to be meek and submissive, they clung to the scriptural mandate found in Acts that it is better to follow God rather than human law, even if it looks "particular," results in people calling them "impudent," or ruptures the bonds of family beyond repair; and their courageous affirmative response to God's call can still stir and inspire us today.

When we examine their own words and the testimony of those who knew them, many of the same qualities recur: deep piety, devotion to prayer, and a burning desire to serve and love God with everything in them. Their wholehearted submission to God empowered them to stand fast even when that meant stepping outside acceptable boundaries for women in order to proclaim the gospel of Jesus Christ. None of them embarked on their unusual ministries in order to make a statement or intending to flout convention; for many, as with Susanna Wesley, it started by leading devotions for their household, which then surprisingly grew into leading worship for a large number of others as well.[7]

Lessons for Us

It is my hope that this book will encourage the people called Methodists, both clergy and laity, to explore these questions and not only to learn *about* these women but to learn *from* them, to find in them wonderful spiritual guides and companions, faithful encouragers and mentors, courageous saints and ministers. As I write these words on All Saints' Day, I encourage today's Methodists to turn our thoughts toward the early Methodist women leaders who are part of that great cloud of witnesses, and to give thanks for their sacrifices, their example, their boldness, and their faith. Truly, these exceptional women deserve to be remembered and honored as "Mothers in Israel."[8]

Susanna Annesley Wesley and the Beginnings of Methodism

Able Divine and Preacher of Righteousness

Any discussion of early Methodist women must start with Susanna Annesley Wesley. Revered as a Methodist icon and heralded as a remarkable woman of her time, scholars differ in their appraisal of her place in the history of Methodism, seeing her primarily as the mother of the Wesleys and even questioning whether or not she was a Methodist. Unconscious of the sexism and condescension in his praise, eighteenth-century Methodist preacher Adam Clarke salutes her as the epitome of the Proverbs 31 woman, rhapsodizing: "If it were not unusual to apply such an epithet to a woman, I would not hesitate to say she was an able divine."[1]

Henry Rack contends that had Susanna lived in another century, she "might have been an able devotional writer or practical theologian,"[2] while Samuel Rogal objects that she was a woman of the late seventeenth and early eighteenth centuries and we can only view her against that backdrop.[3] However, John Newton heralds her as John Wesley's first and most formative teacher, spiritual mentor, and pastor.[4] John Wesley himself wrote upon her death: "I cannot but farther observe that even she (as well as her father and grandfather, her husband, and her three sons) had been, in her measure and degree, a preacher of righteousness."[5]

1

Puritan, Anglican, and Methodist?

The youngest daughter of a prominent Non-Conformist pastor, Susanna Annesley joined the Established Church before she was thirteen years of age. She was therefore undoubtedly a Puritan who turned Anglican, but was she ever a Methodist? While acknowledging that the last years of her life were spent at the very heart of London Methodism, Rogal asserts that those who see her as a "card-carrying" Methodist are indulging in wishful thinking.[6] Conversely, Newton argues that she was the daughter of Puritanism *and* the Mother of Methodism, representing continuity between them, and further that she has a place in the Holy Catholic Church as a saint, bearing "the authentic marks of spiritual greatness upon her."[7] He concludes that she found it "no inconsistency to be a Puritan, an Anglican, and a Methodist, and . . . she is the embodiment of all three of those religious strands."[8]

Whatever one's view, Susanna's imprint can be clearly discerned in her legacy of letters, journals, and educational, catechetical essays. Charles Wallace's edited volume of her complete writings reveals a richer portrait of this extraordinary woman whose breadth and depth of theological and devotional reading *and* insightful reflecting and writing mark her as one of the most learned and pious women of her own—or any—time.[9] Though restrictions placed on her because of her sex barred her from attending Oxford or Cambridge, Susanna was in fact an able devotional writer, a practical theologian and divine, an educator, a spiritual director, a pastor, and a Christian role model. Her spiritual literacy is clearly illustrated in her surviving writings.[10]

Spiritual Director, Educator, Preacher, and Worship Leader

As a spiritual director, Susanna Wesley wrote letters giving sound spiritual advice and theological counsel to her children; and in good Puritan fashion, she kept a personal journal of introspective musings and prayers. As educator and pastor, she devised a commentary on the Decalogue and an exposition on the Apostles' Creed for her children's use. As preacher and worship leader of community-wide prayer meetings and worship, and as educator in her home school classroom, she modeled Christian leadership as a capable, intellectual, devout woman. Late in life, she even wrote an astute anonymous defense of her sons' theology in response to the disagreement over predestination between them and George Whitefield.[11]

Maintaining that Susanna was neither saint, hero, nor victim, Rogal describes her as a woman and mother deserving of her day in history's spotlight "because she worked terribly hard in her attempts to fortify her children with something more than mother's milk and mother's love; she demonstrated to them that order, discipline, and reason could compensate for human error, ill-fortune, and missed opportunities."[12]

In contrast, in highlighting her formative influence on Methodism in its infancy, Wallace lets her distinctive voice be heard. By doing so, he opens the door for us to "discover her to be a competent, practical theologian-educator and a complex and extraordinary woman in her own historical context."[13] Any discussion of the role of women in the earliest days of Methodism is incomplete without examining her life and thoughts, wherein one discovers certain patterns that were common to many of the early female Methodist leaders. Like Susanna, they possessed liberty of conscience, kept devotional journals, acted as spiritual mentors in person and through letters, educated and mothered families (though not necessarily biological ones), and filled the pastoral role by leading worship, praying and testifying publicly, and in some cases, even preaching.

"My Little Liberty of Conscience"

Susanna Annesley was born January 20, 1669, in Spital Yard, Bishopsgate, London, the twenty-fourth or twenty-fifth child of the Reverend Dr. Samuel Annesley and his wife, name unknown.[14] Annesley, known as the "St. Paul of the Non-conformists," was a prominent Puritan pastor who was deprived of his living of St. Giles Cripplegate in 1662 when he and two thousand other priests refused to agree to the Act of Uniformity.[15] Susanna was therefore brought up among Dissenters, where she was free to peruse her father's extensive theological library. Even at a young age, she was drawn to study and reflection on theological matters, eventually exercising her freedom of conscience by leaving her father's religious tradition for which he had suffered so greatly, despite her deep respect for him and all he stood for, when she was not quite thirteen years old.[16] That same liberty of conscience was later profoundly lived out in her interactions with the other significant men in her life and with the church as well.

Though it must have come as a shock, there is no reason to think Samuel Annesley tried to persuade her otherwise, but rather that he respected her independence and encouraged her to follow her own conscience. A dissenting daughter of dissent, Susanna was what we would call today "a liberated woman, because her father was a liberated man."[17] Embracing the church that had caused her father such pain and deprived him of his living before her birth was only done after much reading and serious study, after meditation and careful reflection, a process she later documented in a thoughtful, organized essay that unfortunately has not survived the many years since being written.[18]

In writing to her son Samuel in October 1709, following a February fire that destroyed the family home and nearly cost her son John his life, she describes this lost essay as "an account of the whole transaction, under which head I had included the main of the controversy between them and the Established Church . . . ; and then followed the reasons that determined my judgment to the preference of the Church of England."[19] She had apparently completed most of this record of her reflections as well as a discourse on receiving the sacrament, but the unfortunate blaze that consumed the rectory destroyed these and all her other earliest writings, as well as the numerous manuscripts, papers, and books left to her in her father's will.[20] This fire, the second suffered by the family within seven years, would loom large in Wesley family history and in the story of Methodism.

In 1682 Susanna Annesley probably first met her future husband Samuel Wesley at the wedding of her sister Elizabeth to John Dunton when Samuel was a student training for the Dissenting Ministry.[21] Just as Susanna's pious study and reading were leading her toward joining the Church of England, so too was Samuel being drawn away from Non-Conformity and toward the Established Church. He soon left the academy for Exeter College, Oxford, where he paid his way by acting as a servitor, waiting on students who were better off financially.[22] Upon graduation, he accepted a curacy at St Botolph's, Aldersgate, London, and he and Susanna were married on November 12, 1688, at Marylebone Church, where their son Charles and most of his family would be buried many decades later.[23]

After briefly serving as a navy chaplain, Samuel became the rector of St Leonard's Church, South Ormsby in Lincolnshire, and there he, Susanna, and their infant son Samuel moved in June 1690.[24] During their six-year tenure, more children were born, an almost annual event, and upon moving to Epworth for Samuel to take the living of St Andrew's Church in 1696, they were accompanied by four little ones, leaving three others buried in the graveyard at St Leonard's.[25] Samuel was not gifted at money management, and thus Susanna found herself caught in a cycle of poverty and grief. Additionally, she and Samuel had very different personalities, for while Susanna somehow combined the ability to manage a large household while maintaining an almost monastic life of devotion and discipline, Samuel had little skill at dealing with worldly matters, and as the family grew, so did the debt.[26]

In addition to having a large family and experiencing serious money woes, Susanna and Samuel both held strong political views that did not always coincide. Holding sympathy with the Non-Jurors and believing James II to be the rightful king, she regarded King William III as a usurper of the throne, while Samuel was fervently supportive of the House of Orange. This difference of opinion came to a head one night in 1702 when he noticed that she did not echo his "Amen" to a prayer for the king and called her into his study to ask why. In a letter written to Lady Yarborough, Susanna describes the event:

> I was a little surprised at the question and don't know well what I answered, but too too well I remember what followed: he immediately kneeled down and imprecated the divine Vengeance upon himself and all his posterity if ever he touched me more or came into a bed with me before I had begged God's pardon and his for not saying Amen to the prayer for the King.[27]

In his *Memoirs of the Wesley Family*, Adam Clarke records this episode differently, sharing it as told to him by John Wesley. In this version, when Samuel demanded to know why she did not say amen when he prayed for the king, Susanna responded that she did not believe the Prince of Orange to be the king, to which Samuel indignantly replied that they must part "for if we have *two* Kings, we must have *two beds*."[28] In this version of events, Samuel returned home the following year upon the death of King William because both he and Susanna found mutual agreement on the legitimacy of Queen Anne's right to the throne, and therefore John became the fruits of their reconciliation, born in June 1703.[29]

However, John Wesley and therefore Adam Clarke were mistaken; the episode took much longer to unfold and was far more dire and dramatic than those few sentences indicate.[30] In several letters written during the crisis, Susanna recounts her reasoning and unsuccessful attempts to persuade Samuel to resume marital relations and rectory life with her and their family. One such letter, written to Lady Yarborough, a Yorkshire noblewoman and friend with Nonjuring sympathies, makes her position clear: "I've unsuccessfully represented to him the unlawfulness and unreasonableness of his Oath; that the Man in that case has no more power over his own Body than the Woman over her's; that since I'm willing to let him quietly enjoy his opinions, he ought not to deprive me of my little liberty of conscience."[31]

So strongly did she feel that she frankly reveals to Lady Yarborough that nothing, not even reputation or friends, mattered to her at all in comparison with "preserving a conscience void of offence towards God and man," and she declares she would be mocking almighty God if she were to ask for pardon for what she does not consider sin.[32]

At her request, Lady Yarborough referred the matter to a friend, Nonjuring Suffragan Bishop George Hickes, who agreed that Susanna was in the right. Perhaps encouraged by this, Susanna wrote with further distressing news. Rather than reconciling with her, Samuel determined to return to the sea as a chaplain, leaving Susanna with their six small children, refusing her reasonable suggestion that they put the case to arbitration with two judges, one of his choosing and one of hers.[33] Despite her concern for their children and secondarily for herself, Susanna courageously continued to insist on her right to her own conscience, displaying a sense of complete trust that "the charitable Being that feeds the Ravens and clothes the Lilies" would not cease to care for her or for her little ones.[34]

Susanna demonstrates a remarkable sense of independence of conscience in this matter just as she had shown in her decision to forsake Puritanism for the Church of England. Despite being abandoned by her husband and facing grave hardship and public embarrassment, she insists on her prerogative to hold her own views quite apart from her marital vow of obedience. She repeatedly but unsuccessfully attempts to persuade Samuel of the folly of his oath and the injustice of his orders to simply abandon her own deeply felt allegiances and agree with him, doing all within her power to effect a reconciliation—but without capitulation to his unreasonable demand.

Taking advantage of Samuel's absence, Susanna then wrote to Bishop Hickes herself, sharing her conviction that Samuel was troubled by his oath but would not back down nor admit that he was wrong. She further tells the bishop that Samuel's suggestion of referring the matter to the bishop of Lincoln and the archbishop of York is unhelpful because she feels she cannot expect a fair hearing from either of them and that Samuel grandly asserts that he cannot live with someone who is the enemy of his country, which he feels obligated to love above anything else in the world. She then candidly concedes: "If I thought or could be persuaded that I'm in an error I would freely retract it and ask his pardon before the whole world. He accuses me of pride and of obstinacy and insists upon my making satisfaction for the injury he believes I have done him. I dare not plead guilty to such an Indictment, but yet I hope however I may in other instances be culpable, in this I'm pretty innocent."[35]

Bishop Hickes responded to her letter, strongly condemning Samuel's rash oath as "perjury" and as being "wholly contrary to the prior obligation of his marriage-promise."[36] He encourages her to "stick to God and your conscience which are your best friends, whatever you may suffer for adhering to them."[37] Adding his prayers that Samuel would be converted and enabled to "follow the blessed life of the meek and charitable Jesus," Bishop Hickes concludes with an assurance of his support and friendship.[38]

Meanwhile, a fellow minister unexpectedly encountered Samuel, dissuading him from following through with his plans to run away to sea, despite taking Samuel's side in the matter.[39] This was not, however, the end of the family's woes, for as Susanna later wrote to Bishop Hickes, the rectory caught on fire (the first of two within a span of seven years) and even their belongings that did not burn were nevertheless ruined.[40] This 1702 tragic loss of property seems to have opened Samuel's eyes and shocked him into wondering if his rash curse upon his posterity was being fulfilled.[41] Providentially, the couple reconciled and resumed marital relations, resulting in the birth of their son John, known to the family as "Jacky," in June of the following year.[42]

Rebuilding commenced and life resumed a predictable round of pregnancy, childbirth, hostility from Samuel's parishioners, the death of several of her little ones, education of her surviving children (both female and male), and the ever-present specter of financial debt. On one occasion, Samuel's creditor had him consigned to debtors' prison in Lincoln, and when Susanna sent him her wedding ring to sell, he promptly returned it to her and begged the archbishop of York for financial help.[43]

"Doing Good to Their Souls"

Foolishly, in view of the never-ending burden of debt, Samuel delighted in traveling to London on behalf of his diocese for Convocation, though it cost £150 that his family could ill afford.[44] He seems to have leapt at the opportunity to escape the gloom of his rural parish and the noise of his large family for the glamourous, intellectually stimulating life of London. He likely hoped this might improve his chances to secure a more comfortable ministry setting.[45] If so, his hopes were to be dashed. His only financial gains came in the form of charity, and he remained the rector in Epworth, and later Wroot, until his death in 1735.

Since Samuel was often away, the family had little money; and since she was often unwell, there was little in Susanna's life over which she could exercise control except the raising and educating of her children, which she accomplished by establishing a home school and teaching them herself. Through her loving though rigorous educational and religious training, Susanna Wesley infused them with "a disciplined attention to scriptural and religious education, attendance upon their prayers, and a practical education focused on literacy and writing."[46]

Daily lessons followed regular school hours during which interruptions were not allowed between the morning hours of nine and twelve nor from two to five in the afternoon. There was little time for play or recreation in this scheme of instruction. Susanna directed her energy and intellectual power toward educating her children with a combination of "the practices of literacy with the growth of spirituality."[47]

In her letters, catechetical writings, and private journal, Susanna reveals herself as a devoted parent and a tough spiritual director who wrestles with the call to lovingly nurture her children and the need to surrender them to the care of a God whose ways are often inexplicable. These themes would recur throughout her life, influencing the theology of her sons, "and it is no surprise that love became the core of Methodist spirituality."[48] Through her loving though rigorous educational and religious training of her children, Susanna Wesley infused them with "a disciplined attention to scriptural and religious education, attendance upon their prayers, and a practical education focused on literacy and writing."[49]

Not surprisingly, she drew upon a wide range of sources, including John Locke, her Puritan upbringing, and the Bible. Arising from her childhood experience in a Puritan household, which combined discipline and devotion with study and reflection, these educational principles as practiced with her own children might well be described as loving but strict.[50] She sought to combine natural maternal affection with a method of discipline and order, believing that adherence to parental authority was the first step toward teaching a child to respect and honor God. To do otherwise was to do the devil's work for him. [51]

As their chief educator, Susanna devised eight principal rules by which she molded the minds and formed the characters of her children, and Locke's influence is discernible. Beginning with her first child, Samuel, she created a methodical means by which her children began to learn the alphabet on their fifth birthdays and then to read from the book of Genesis. Most importantly, however, she employed her time to ensure that they were "prayerfully educated in the things of God." Those words can be seen inscribed on a memorial plaque at Wesley Church, Epworth, a lasting and loving tribute to the success of her efforts.

Her letter of October 11, 1709, to son Samuel ("Sammy") who was a student at Westminster and later at Christ Church, Oxford, is emblematic of her aims. She writes that her main desire is to "do some small service to my children, that, as I have brought 'em into the world, so that it might please God to make me (though unworthy) an instrument of doing good to their souls."[52]

Susanna's educational system so impressed her son John that as an adult he requested a detailed account of her household regimen and child-rearing practices to which she responded in a letter of July 24, 1732.[53] At first she demurred, feeling that her methods could not be of use to anyone else and that few mothers would be able or willing to devote twenty years of their lives to follow such a disciplined system aimed at saving her children's souls or lead such a "retiring" life as hers.[54] However, she eventually acquiesced and penned a remarkable account of her educational method and rationale for it. In particular, she sets it in the context of preparing her children to submit to the will of God by first conquering their wills and bringing them to an obedient temper. She was convinced that when the reason and piety of the parents governed the child, the principles of true religion would then be firmly established in the child's mind.[55]

Not surprisingly and almost certainly of necessity, her brood of children were from infancy put in a "regular way of living," in which they learned quickly "to fear the rod" and cry softly, a practice she likely adopted in order to protect her little ones from their father's quick temper.[56] It appears that Samuel was an impatient and reserved authority figure to be respected and sometimes feared, and that Susanna became the central focus for the children's affection.[57]

Unlike most other women of her time, Susanna was well-read and independent, so the eighth pillar of her educational platform is not shocking—she absolutely refused to teach her daughters the usual domestic arts before they were able to read well. "This rule also is much to be observed; for the putting children to learn sewing before they can read perfectly is the very reason why so few women can read fit to be heard, and never to be well understood."[58] Her emphasis on educating her daughters as well as her sons was unusual in a time when no college or university education was open to them, and she made every attempt to prepare them for the challenges of a male-dominated world "by endowing them with good habits, firm principles, and a deep religious faith, and she maintained this role by correspondence long after they left home."[59] Their letters indicate a loving, respectful relationship, but the paths the Wesley daughters trod as adults were hard, and even the warmest of maternal love and care could not protect them from heartbreak and grief.

"You Writ This Sermon for Hetty"

Susanna's lasting influence and generally positive relationships with her children well into adulthood far exceeded theirs with their father, whose improvidence with money and implacable sense of righteousness caused much heartache for them all, perhaps most particularly to Mehetabel, known in the family as Hetty. In 1726, when she eloped and became pregnant out of wedlock, her lover dropped her, leaving her no choice but to return home to her angry and disappointed parents and then contract an unhappy marriage to a near stranger at Samuel's insistence. His fury never fully abated, and he apparently never believed her repentance to be genuine. In response to one tear-stained missive in which Hetty sought to re-establish a relationship with him, Samuel praises her husband for "his civilities" to her and coolly concludes with harsh words: "Restrain your wit if you wish to write again, and I will answer your next if I like it."[60] Even though she swallowed her pride and deep hurt and wrote to him again, there is no record of his response, if he even responded at all.

In his efforts to intercede for Hetty, John brought down some of their father's wrath on himself by preaching a sermon on charity at the Wroot church on August 26, 1726, in which he clearly alluded to Samuel's harsh treatment of Hetty without naming either of them outright. Rather than discussing it directly with John, the furious Samuel instead complained in a letter to his eldest son Sammy, who chastised John, not only for his "charitable" attitude toward Hetty but also for a perceived failure to repay certain debts incurred in the course of his Oxford education.[61] John's response in a letter of December 5–6, 1726, is a reasonable refutation of the points of dispute, shedding light on the depth of insight that Susanna had with regard to her children's actions and motivations. After fully explaining his own side of the disagreement between himself and their father and informing Sammy that their mother had read the sermon before it was preached, John writes:

> My sister Hetty's behavior has, for aught I have heard, been innocent enough since her marriage. Most of my disputes with my father were on her account, he being inconceivably exasperated against her. 'Tis likely enough he would not see her when at Wroot; he has disowned her long ago, and never spoke of her in my hearing but with the utmost

detestation. Both he, my mother, and several of my sisters were persuaded her penitence was but feigned. One great reason for my writing the above-mentioned sermon was to endeavor, as far [as] in me lay, to convince them that even on supposit[ion] that she was impenitent some tenderness was due to her still; which my mother when I read it to her was so well aware of that she told me as soon as I had read it, "You writ this sermon for Hetty; the rest was brought in for the sake of the last paragraph."[62]

Though Samuel refused to ever forgive Hetty, she and Susanna did eventually reconcile and became particularly affectionate toward each other after Samuel's death.[63]

Because of their childhood exposure to this atmosphere of pious and intelligent femininity demonstrated by their insightful mother, it is not surprising that John and Charles Wesley had a high regard for women's abilities and intelligence as well as for their capacity for leadership in a religious setting. John's response to Sister Hetty's disgrace and sad married life made him especially sensitive to women in similar circumstances and may explain his later friendship and encouragement for Sarah Ryan, whom he appointed housekeeper at the New Room in Bristol.

Sarah had been married to three different men who all abandoned her without bothering to legally divorce her, and her life and legacy were tainted by the negative assessments of those, including John Wesley's wife, Molly, who refused to acknowledge her changed life after her conversion and the ministry to which she was called. However, despite her questionable marital history, she became a respected Methodist class leader and one of the earliest female preachers. The office of housekeeper was important, requiring managerial skills and entailing serious spiritual responsibilities, and Sarah Ryan, in her role as housekeeper at the New Room in Bristol, regarded offering hospitality and keeping order in her "family" important aspects of her vocation.[64]

"Some Method in Instructing and Writing"

Believing her vocation as mother, educator, and spiritual guide carried eternal implications for the souls of her young ones, Susanna's work with them was grounded in prayer. Her conviction of the importance of continual prayer undergirded all that she did. The entry in her personal devotional journal for the evening of May 24, 1711, is indicative of the depth of her commitment and the comprehensive nature of her approach: "'Tis necessary to observe some method in instructing and writing for your children. Go through your brief exposition on the Ten Commandments, which are a summary of the moral law. Then briefly explain the principles of revealed religion, which will make up the second letter. Subjoin by way of essay a short discourse on the being and attributes of God."[65]

Her next entry further underlines her reliance upon God through prayer: "When you feel yourself afflicted by pain, sickness, or any other uneasiness, the first thing you do, make an act of submission to the will of God."[66] This rule undergirded her entire educational enterprise. As a result, her children learned as toddlers that the Sabbath day was different from the rest of the week and, while at family prayer, were taught to sign for a parental blessing even before they were able to kneel or speak. As soon as they could speak, she taught them the Lord's Prayer, which they recited every morning and evening, and as they grew older, they learned a short catechism, prayers for their parents, verses of scripture, and some of the collects from the *Book of Common Prayer*.[67] Additionally, they were not permitted to eat snacks between meals or to address the servants rudely; they ate whatever food was put in front of them without complaint, and they called one another "Brother" or "Sister" followed by the sibling's name.[68]

Susanna expected and obtained her children's obedience, but if they were "charged with a fault, of which they were guilty, if they would ingenuously confess it, and promise to amend," they were not punished. In a letter to John, she offers a cryptic criticism of her husband, stating that this practice precluded a lot of lying and would have prevented even more had "one in the family . . . observed it."

However, Samuel could not be convinced of the common sense of this rule and as a result was often the recipient of colorful stories and equivocations, which could have been avoided if he had dealt more kindly with the erring child in the first place. She believed that no child should be beat twice for the same fault and that if the erring child repented of it, she or he should not be reproached with it again.[69]

All of this took a tremendous commitment of time and nearly infinite patience. It is said that Samuel Wesley overheard her teaching one of the children the same thing over and over, and his low reserves of tolerance ran out, whereupon he asked her in exasperation how she could bear to teach the same lesson twenty times in a row. Being of an unruffled disposition, she calmly replied that it was the twentieth repetition that crowned the rest and that without it, all her efforts would have been for naught.[70] She was, however, a human being and not an angel, so naturally there were times when her children tried her patience. In her private devotional journal, after apparently responding irritably to one of the children, Susanna chides herself:

> Never correct your children to satisfy your passions, but out of a sense of your duty to reclaim them from their errors, and to preserve your authority. And then be exceeding careful to let the measure of correction, be proportionable to the fault. Make great allowances for the weakness of their reason, and immaturity of their judgments, but never spare them through foolish fondness when they sin against God.[71]

It is likely that her inclusion of the admonition against letting "foolish fondness" keep her from exercising parental discipline indicates that she found a tendency within herself to do so, a temptation common to many loving parents.[72]

"My Tenderest Regard Is for Your Immortal Soul and Its Eternal Happiness"

After the 1709 fire, the children were dispersed until their home was habitable. As pastor and spiritual director of her family, Susanna modeled the importance of letter-writing as a means of providing spiritual guidance and theological conversation.[73] The written word, in the form of both letters and extended essays, was an essential means of continuing her scattered children's devotional nurture, just as it had been with Sammy when he was away at school.[74] Her guidance was much respected and sought after, and her letters are models of offering spiritual direction by giving both practical and theological advice. Lovingly but firmly she unhesitatingly called her children out if necessary, using her own experience and faith as a guide.

In one such letter to Sammy written November 27, 1707, she seeks to guide him with regard to resisting temptation. Combining common sense, theological insight, and maternal intuition, she provides incomparable spiritual guidance and pastoral care. First, she reminds him of the fallen nature of all humankind, admonishing him to become aware of what kind of temptation most troubles him, noting that Satan turns our own weapons of our "corrupted faculties and appetites" against us. She points out that this may take the form of tempting Sammy to neglect prayer and praise of God or producing sinful or unnecessary thoughts as he attempts to go about his religious duties. Knowing her son's temperament so well, she shrewdly asserts that his most likely temptations are of impurity and "intemperance in meat, drink, or recreation." To combat these impure thoughts or actions in situations when a lengthy prayer time is not possible, she recommends sincere, quick "ejaculations" of prayer and a constant sense of the omnipresence of God.[75]

She also covers the issue of peer pressure, astutely addressing the "fear of being thought singular and precise" and being laughed at for refusing to do what everyone else is doing:

> To this I shall only say, remember what you are, a Christian, the disciple of a crucified Jesus—and he has commanded that all his disciples should take up the cross and follow him. Consider how "he made himself of no reputation," but "was despised and rejected of men," and therefore how little reason have you to regard the unjust censures of a mistaken

world or being made the subject of a little raillery because you will not be ashamed of or deny your Master.[76]

In conclusion, she addresses the matter of temperance in recreation, acknowledging that he certainly does need to take time for exercise but that he has a better sense of how much time his schedule will allow for it, wisely adding,

> You best know whether your heart be too much set upon it. If it be, I'll tell you what rule I observed in the same case, when I was young and too much addicted to childish diversions, which was this: never to spend more time in any matter of mere recreation in one day than I spent in private religious duties. I leave it to your consideration whether this is practicable by you or no. I think it is.[77]

Having been unwell and in pain while writing to him, she declares that she will forego responding to his request about preparing to receive the Sacrament until she hears from him again, closing with a final word of blessing.

Likewise, after the 1709 fire, Susanna was determined to continue the spiritual nurture of her daughters through her letters and long essays since they currently had no other way of conversing and no hint of when they would be reunited. In the October 1709 letter to Sammy several months after the second rectory fire, she lamented that the little manual she had been assembling as a means of instructing and guiding her children had perished in the flames, because she felt it would have been useful for all of her children, sons and daughters alike. Undaunted, however, and committed to doing all she could to nourish their souls, she embarked once again on the task of catechesis, composing an exposition on the Apostles' Creed and later one on the Ten Commandments that was unfortunately never completed.[78]

Concerned for her daughter Suky's well-being, most especially with regard to her spiritual health here on earth and in the life to come, she turned her hand to composing an essay on the Apostles' Creed:

Since our misfortunes have separated us from each other, and we can no longer enjoy the opportunities we once had of conversing together, I can no other way discharge the duty of a parent or comply with my inclination of doing you all the good I can, but by writing. You know very well how I love you. I love your body and do earnestly beseech Almighty God to bless it with health and all things necessary for its comfort and support in this world. But my tenderest regard is for your immortal soul and its eternal happiness; which regard I cannot better express than by endeavoring to instil into your mind those principles of knowledge and virtue that are absolutely necessary in order to your leading a good life here, which is the only thing that can infallibly secure your happiness hereafter.[79]

Her goal in composing this letter with its extended essay on the Apostles' Creed was to provide a good foundation so that Suky might claim her Christian faith for herself and not simply because she was an inhabitant of an ostensibly Christian nation or because her parents professed it. For Suky to profess to be a Christian for those reasons or simply to advance her position in the eyes of the world would mean that she would "never be able to stand in the day of temptation" nor "ever enter into the kingdom of heaven." Ever practical, Susanna recommends that Suky keep the letter for future reference since she might not be able at present to fully comprehend everything it contains. Painstakingly, she works her way through the Creed, phrase by phrase, and at the end of her discussion of "the life everlasting" she overflows in praise: "Oh blessed grace. Mysterious love. How shall we then adore and praise what we cannot here apprehend aright. How will love and joy work in the soul. But I cannot express it—I cannot conceive it."[80]

Additionally, Susanna mentions that she has been busily preparing other discourses, essays examining "the being of God, the divine authority of scripture, the truth of revealed religion, [and] a future judgment," to be completed when she has more leisure time. Adding a few further paragraphs on the fallen nature of humankind, she closes by assuring Suky of her prayers for God to enlighten Suky's mind and to renew and sanctify her by the Spirit so that she may become a child of God by adoption and an heir of the kingdom in the world to come.[81]

Susanna apparently also shared a copy of this discussion of the Creed with son Sammy, reminding him that she regarded the best employment of her time to be in writing things that will be useful for her children. Admitting that there are many good books they could consult for fuller treatments of these subjects, Susanna believes that her children will nevertheless highly value her words, realizing they come from "their mother, who is perhaps more concerned for their eternal happiness than anyone in the world," and she encourages Sammy to carefully read the papers she sends to him, even if it is only so he can compose something better.[82]

Feeling a serious call to provide instruction for her scattered offspring, Susanna persisted in writing these discourses, despite feeling herself ill-equipped for the task and despite a lack of support from her rector husband. However diffident she may have felt, she nevertheless was a woman of strong and informed opinions, and she possessed not only a sense of duty in her role as their spiritual mentor but also a sense of her own self that "allows her not only to love and support her family but also to advise, teach, argue with, and sometimes stubbornly resist even her husband, brother, and sons."[83] She might best be viewed as a sort of bridge figure who is paradoxically neither "the somewhat tamed successor of Puritan prophetesses" nor "the hopeful predecessor of women freed by the eighteenth century revival" and yet somehow is both.[84]

"Yet Do I Very Well Know What It Is to Rejoice in the Midst of Deep Affliction"

Upon their eventual homecoming to the newly rebuilt red brick rectory, Susanna was dismayed to find that much of her careful teaching had fallen by the wayside, her children's manners had deteriorated, they were neglecting the Sabbath, and they were acquiring an accent that grated on her London-bred ears.[85] To counter this reversal of her hard work, she developed a schedule to insure that she spent some time one-on-one with each child every week to discuss whatever was most pressing on her or his mind. This ongoing concern for each child's unique needs is evident in the correspondence between her and her sons when they were away at school and even when they were ordained to the priesthood as well as her letters to her daughters.[86]

Prayerfully reflecting in her journal, Susanna resolves to dedicate the balance of her life to God's service, especially as spiritual guide and mother. An evening entry on May 17, 1711, with the initials "S.J." written beside the date is assumed to mean her son John, particularly since that date fell on a Thursday, the day specifically set aside for one-to-one time with him. Referring to his providential escape from a fiery death, she writes: "And I do intend to be more particularly careful of the soul of this child that thou has so mercifully provided for than ever I have been, that I may do my endeavour to instill into his mind the principles of thy true religion and virtue. Lord, give me grace to do it sincerely and prudently, and bless my attempts with good success."[87]

In a letter dated February 6, 1712, she writes to her husband Samuel as he was attending Convocation in London yet again: "On Monday I talk with Molly, on Tuesday with Hetty, Wednesday with Nancy, Thursday with Jacky, Friday with Patty, Saturday with Charles, and with Emily and Sukey together on Sunday."[88] (Sammy was at Oxford by this time, and Kezzy, the youngest of her children, was a toddler.) Her practice of meeting alone with her children provided a model of the impact of intimate spiritual conversation and guidance, a lesson that was not lost on her son John when the Methodist movement began to grow and spread.[89] It is possible to see her influence on his later attention to Christian Conferencing as a means of grace, in part because of this careful individual attention paid to her children.

Her dedication of time to each child individually and the pious, intellectual example she set for them so influenced her son John that even as a Fellow of Lincoln College, he did not hesitate to ask for her advice or opinion on theological and spiritual matters as well as for her prayers, nor did she hesitate to share her thoughts with him. He readily turned to her not simply because she was his mother but because she was wise, well-read, and pious. In a letter to him written June 8, 1725, she gives voice to her deep faith and conviction of the goodness of God in the midst of poverty, death, and sadness.

> 'Tis stupid to say nothing is an affliction to a good man. . . .
> Nor do I understand how any man can thank God for present misery. Yet do I very well know what it is to rejoice in the midst of deep affliction: not in the affliction itself, for then it must necessarily cease to be one. But in this [we may rejoice], that we are in the hand of a God who never did, nor ever can exert his power in an act of oppression, injustice, or cruelty. In the power of that superior wisdom which disposes all events and has promised that all things shall work together for good (for the spiritual and eternal good) of those that love him. We may rejoice in hope that Almighty Goodness "will not suffer us to be tempted above what we are able, but will with the temptations make a way to escape, [that we may be able to bear it]." In a word, we may and ought to rejoice that God has assured us he will never leave or forsake us; but if we continue faithful to him, he will take care to conduct us safely through all the changes and chances of this mortal life to those blessed regions of joy and immortality where sorrow and sin can never enter.[90]

This made a lasting impression on John, as seen in his sermon "Free Grace" that signaled a public split between him and George Whitefield over the doctrine of election.

> For there are many Scriptures the true sense whereof neither you nor I shall know till death is swallowed up in victory. But this I know, better it were to say it had no sense at all than to say it had such a sense as this. It cannot mean,

whatever it mean besides, that the God of truth is a liar. Let it mean what it will, it cannot mean that the Judge of all the world is unjust. No Scripture can mean that God is not love, or that his mercy is not over all his works. That is, whatever it prove beside, no Scripture can prove predestination.[91]

As noted, John Wesley so valued his mother's example of faith and her method of child-rearing that he requested that she compose an essay for him to share with others. When she initially questioned this, emphasizing her retirement from the world, he responded with a letter in which he expresses a desire also to renounce the world and trustingly asks her the best way to go about it for himself.

> In many things you have interceded for me and prevailed. Who knows but in this too you may be successful? If you can spare me only that little part of Thursday evening which you formerly bestowed upon me in another manner, I doubt not but it would be as useful now for correcting my heart as it was then for the forming my judgment.[92]

In a letter to Charles written on December 6, 1738, she freely offers her theological perspective as she addresses the question of whether or not a person must be able to pinpoint an exact moment of spiritual awakening, rejecting the notion that "one size fits all."

> I do not judge it necessary for us to know the precise time of our conversion. 'Tis sufficient if we have a reasonable hope that we are passed from death to life by the fruits of the Holy Spirit wrought in our hearts. Such are repentance, faith, hope, love, etc. Our Lord acts in various ways and by various means on different tempers, nor is the work of regeneration begun and perfected at once. Others (rarely too) have been sanctified from the womb, and like Obadiah, have served the Lord from their youth. But from these exempt cases we can draw no general rules, nor ought we too curiously to search after the knowledge of the operations of God's Holy Spirit. His ways are past finding out.[93]

"A Devout and Serious Temper of Mind in the Midst of Much Worldly Business"

It appears that both necessity and Susanna's own personality lent themselves to the establishment of a structured rhythm of life for her children and for herself, as well as a pattern of devotional time that included keeping a diary. A child of the Puritans, she developed a rich interior life of communion with God through her spiritual journal that reflects her commitment to times of meditation and reflection in the morning, at noon, and in the evening.[94] In one entry, she addresses this resolution to spend at least one hour each morning and evening in private devotions and concludes that while sickness and unavoidable business has sometimes made her shorten them, she has not deliberately omitted or shortened those times set apart for God and that she actually tends to exceed the time allotted. This leads not to self-congratulation but to further praise, "Glory be to thee, O Lord."[95] No mere exercise in detailing daily life, Susanna's journal was foundational to her devotional life. It was not simply an accounting of spiritual ups and downs; it was a "means of grace," as it would be for her sons and later Methodists as well.[96]

To preserve a sense of modesty, her wide-ranging journal entries are at times written in veiled language and in the second person. She gives herself advice just as she might dispense it to someone else. Entries include insightful comments on books she was reading, thoughts on educating her children and caring for their souls, and reflections on her own spiritual struggles.[97] She can be sharply self-critical in her pursuit of holiness of heart and life, but she is not above boldly trying to bargain with God in the style of the patriarch Jacob. Reflecting on the never-ending financial hardship of her family, she writes:

> I had been many years under very heavy pressures, which by their continuance and increase grew almost intolerable, nor could I enjoy any ease or composure of mind till God's good Spirit put it into my heart peremptorily to resolve that, in obedience to Jesus Christ, I would never give way to

any anxiety of mind about the things of this world, let what would happen.[98]

Upon further reflection, she concludes that she has been faithful to her end of the bargain despite sometimes still experiencing the "dead weight" of sadness and a feeling of perplexity at the ongoing adversity of her life, and she sees clear parallels between Jacob going into a land of idolaters and herself trying to live as a Christian in a country where even professed Christians idolize their own wit or strength or learning or beauty.[99] Throughout her life, she does, however, find strength in her regular spiritual practices, as in keeping this prayer journal. When her health fails and she experiences great bodily pain, she clings to hope in God's wisdom and mercy and offers her whole being to God without necessarily requesting deliverance from her difficulties.[100]

As the mother to many children and mistress of a busy household, it is not surprising that she muses on the challenges of keeping to a regular pattern of devotional practice and of maintaining a state of mind firmly fixed on God when there are so many worldly matters and pressing concerns to attend to:

> Tis, perhaps, one of the most difficult things in the world to preserve a devout and serious temper of mind in the midst of much worldly business, and therefore I would advise that no person voluntarily involve themselves in or take upon them the management of more business than they can throw into such a method as may not distract their thoughts or take up too much their time which was given us to work out our salvation. But where a numerous family and a narrow fortune oblige to it, it is not be declined, lest we break the order of providence, and therefore in such a case we must do as a wise workman that takes a piece of work by the great upon hard terms; we must work so much harder, we must be careful to redeem time from sleep, eating, dressing, unnecessary visits, and trifling conversation, that we not be forced to contract our private devotions into

such a little space as may deprive us of the benefit and comforts of them.[101]

She continues in the same vein, often mentioning her own suffering and ill health, not as a matter of complaint but again in order to express her desire to commit herself wholeheartedly to God. However, she is realistic enough to realize that even if she had more leisure time, she might not actually devote more of it to prayer and meditation upon scripture:

> Were I permitted to choose a state of life or positively to ask of God anything in this world, I would humbly choose and beg that I might be placed in such a station wherein I might have daily bread with moderate care without so much hurry and distraction; and that I might have more leisure to retire from the world without injuring my [husband] or children. Nor should any consideration of interest, of riches, honor, pleasure prevail upon me to encumber myself with such a multiplicity of business as I now submit to only in obedience to the order of divine providence.
>
> This is my present thoughts [sic], but yet I do not know whether such a state of life would really be best for me. Nor am I assured that, if I had more leisure, I should be more zealously devoted to God and serve him better than now. Perhaps there might be as many temptations in a quiet and private life as there is in this, or suppose there should not, yet how can I tell but that a constant state of suffering may be necessary to purify the mind and to keep a check upon it, lest it run into vanity, worldly regards, etc., which ought carefully to be avoided, and possibly such a proportion of punishment for some sins is necessary in this life, or otherwise we should not escape punishment hereafter.[102]

Discipline of the self plays a large role in her spiritual life and is reflected in these and other entries. Though she does not often spell out the specific sins that cause her concern, she does occasionally mention particular issues. In one morning reflection, she addresses herself with disapproval at drinking more than one cup of ale in a short time even though it does not break a vow she has made concerning alcohol consumption. She rejoices that God has created her with a body that will not easily allow her to drink excessively, and she considers this an occasion for praise.[103] Some seven years later, she reexamines her vow to not drink more than two glasses of strong liquor at one time, despite Samuel's immediate move to absolve her from such strict discipline, and she again rejoices that she has kept this vow even when others have pressed her to exceed her self-imposed limit. She immediately gives God the glory for this grace rather than patting herself on the back, reminding herself that she is "nothing but corruption and misery" and that if she is enabled to do good or to resist temptation, she ought to always praise God for the undeserved grace to do so.[104]

Independent and strong, Susanna is no revolutionary; her battles with "the world" were not attempts to reform society at large. However, as we have seen, her strong sense of self empowered her "not only to love and support her family but also to advise, teach, argue with, and sometimes stubbornly resist even her husband, brother, and sons."[105] When her clergymen sons Charles and John became convinced of the necessity of having an assurance of justifying faith and declared that they had not truly been Christians until such an experience occurred, she did not hesitate to express her opinion that this new understanding is wrong and illogical. In a letter to Charles dated December 6, 1738, following his "conversion," she writes:

> I think you are fallen into an odd way of thinking. You say that till within a few months you had no spiritual life nor any justifying faith. Now this is as if a man should affirm he was not alive in his infancy, because, when an infant he did not know he was alive. A strange way of arguing, this. Do you not consider that there's some analogy in spiritual to natural life? A man must first be born and then pass through the several stages of infancy, childhood, and youth, before attain to maturity. So Christians are first born

of water and the spirit and then go through many degrees of grace, be first infants, or babes in Christ, as St. Paul calls them, before they become strong Christians. For spiritual strength is the work of time, as well as of God's Holy Spirit. All then that I can gather from your letter is that till a little while ago you were not so well satisfied of your being a Christian as you are now. I heartily rejoice that you have now attained to a strong and lively hope in God's mercy through Christ. Not that I can think you were totally without saving faith before, but then 'tis one thing to have faith and another thing to be sensible that we have it. Faith is the fruit of the Spirit and is the gift of God, but to feel or be inwardly sensible that we have true faith requires a further operation of God's Holy Spirit.[106]

In applying scripture to her own life and tending to her interior life through her journal, Susanna was emboldened to push against the accepted norms and boundaries of acceptable female behavior. Her conscience was carefully nurtured in the richness of her devotional life, enabling her to seem to acquiesce with the restrictions placed upon her as a woman while actually standing her ground and even powerfully resisting.[107] Later Methodist women would also discover that submitting to God's authority rather than to temporal or even ecclesiastical authorities would lead them to understand that their call to ministry and exercise of their talents might even lie outside the home, despite the disapproval of family, friends, and the church itself.[108]

"For That Will Not Satisfy My Conscience"

In many ways, Susanna was like the Mother Superior of her own little spiritual community, engaging in individual direction, writing letters and expositions on spiritual subjects, and educating her children in "the things of God," fueled by her fierce maternal love for her children.[109] Perhaps not surprisingly, her deep love of God and sense of vocation in her role as pastor to her family eventually took on added dimensions within the Epworth community when Samuel was away in London for Convocation during the winter of 1710–1711.[110] Also perhaps not surprisingly, the initiative she displayed led to marital conflict again as her sense of vocation and individual conscience resulted in actions that superseded society's view of a woman's accepted role, both in relation to leadership in worship and her proper place as a wife.

Samuel's frequent absences due to his attendance at Convocation exacerbated the family's financial burden and on this notable occasion left the spiritual welfare of the parish largely in the hands of a not particularly gifted curate named Godfrey Inman who was paid to preach and to lead morning and evening prayers.[111] However, while he was away, partly due to Inman's dull worship leadership and lackluster preaching and partly because of reading an account of the work of Danish missionaries in North America, Susanna felt a heightened sense of responsibility for the souls within her care. In addition to individual meetings with her children, Sunday evenings took on increased importance as a special time of family devotions and worship during which she led the prayers, read sermons, and discussed various spiritual topics.[112]

This was not in and of itself controversial as long as it remained a family devotional practice, but soon Susanna's pastoral care of her family extended beyond her own household, and her neighbors began clamoring to attend as well. Numbers increased rapidly, and eventually some of these parishioners even began to neglect attendance at morning prayer, which prompted the incensed Inman to complain to Samuel that she was leading an illegal conventicle. Inman apparently convinced Samuel that these prayer meetings were, in fact, conventicles, gatherings in defiance of the Act of Toleration of 1689, which led to a spirited exchange of strongly worded letters between Susanna and Samuel.[113] In her letters, Susanna cleverly holds in tension the conventional expectations of a woman of her station and an obedient wife with her strong conviction of the rightness of her unusual actions in what Wallace calls "a fascinating balance of deference and defiance."[114]

To his first reproachful letter, she responded with hers of February 6, which answers his objections point by point—first, the Sunday evening meetings looked particular (peculiar); second, that her sex was an issue as the leader of such gatherings; and third, that the entire matter might reflect badly upon him. In a manner that foreshadows John Wesley's submission to be "more vile" by embarking on field preaching in 1738 and the later unconventional activities of other devout women experiencing a call to publicly proclaim the gospel, she writes, "As to it looking particular, I grant it does, and so does almost everything that is serious or that may in any way advance the glory of God or the salvation of souls, if it be performed out of a pulpit, or in the way of common conversation."[115]

She continues, addressing his second objection by explaining that she is not only a woman but also the mistress of a large family and that she looks upon each of those souls as talents entrusted to her by God while Samuel is absent. She then asks, "And if I am unfaithful to him or to you in neglecting to improve these talents, how shall I answer unto him, when he shall command me to render an account of my stewardship?"[116] She further explains that this practice developed almost accidentally as she sought to make better use of her own time and the time of those around her by offering them an opportunity for afternoon prayers on the Sabbath. Sharing her excitement over the labors of the Danish missionaries, she tells him that she could not refrain from giving God praise for inspiring their efforts to advance the gospel and could talk of almost nothing else for several days. Feeling inspired herself and hoping to do something similar in her own setting, she writes, "At last it came into my mind, though I am not a man nor a minister of the gospel, and so cannot be employed in such a worthy employment as they were; yet . . . I might do somewhat more than I do. . . . I might pray more for the people and speak with more warmth to those with whom I have an opportunity of conversing."[117]

Reminding him of her scheme of meeting with each of their children individually during the week, she explains that these gatherings started out in much the same way, with her speaking to whoever came "more freely and affectionately than before" and with her reading "awakening" sermons with them. Word got out, and more and more people asked to come; and she felt she could not turn them away, and numbers continued to grow. "Last Sunday I believe we had above two hundred, and yet many went away for want of room." Small wonder that Inman was jealous. One might wonder if Samuel himself was a bit envious as well, as he was taken aback by his wife's ability to touch people's hearts with the gospel in ways that he could not. Susanna modestly refrains from declaring outright that God is making use of her talents to do good for their neighbors, saying only that it *might* be the case because with God all things are possible. Without making judgment about whether or not her efforts are succeeding, she addresses his third objection concerning how her undertakings might reflect badly upon Samuel. She points out that these little meetings are not gossip sessions or garden-variety visits but rather times during which she reads a sermon, they sing psalms, and then everyone goes home. She rhetorically asks him why it should scandalize anyone that the wife of the rector should attempt to encourage people to attend church and spend time in prayer rather than in profane activities upon the Lord's Day, proclaiming that she wishes he would not listen if there are complaints because she herself has "long since shook hands with the world, and I heartily wish I had never given them more reason to speak against me."[118]

In his letter, Samuel had apparently suggested that she find a man to read the prayers and sermons during these prayer meetings, but she points out most of the men cannot read well and that no one in their family has a voice that can project strongly enough for everyone to hear. She does worry, however, that it might not be proper for her to lead the prayers in this public setting because she is a woman, but she reports that she did so on at least one occasion because they begged her not to dismiss them before leading them in prayer. This may have mollified Samuel into giving his reluctant approval, but an angry missive from Inman provoked Samuel to write a more strongly worded letter to Susanna about her activities. He wrote to her, this time apparently instructing her to curtail the meetings.[119]

After giving both of them a few days to cool off, she wrote back to him on February 25, 1711, expressing her disappointment that he would allow the complaints of a few people to make him forbid something he had formerly approved. She informs him that she will explain herself once again, though she fears he will disregard it just as he clearly did the last time. With some wit, she muses that some of Inman's disapproval stems from her reading sermons that are better than his. She has heard no outcry from anyone else and has in fact seen not only an increase in church attendance since her gatherings began but also more cordial relations between the parishioners and the rectory family. Additionally many of those who used to waste time playing in the streets on the Sabbath are now more inclined to come hear a good sermon, which must surely be more pleasing to God than their former behavior.

Asking him to judge as impartially as possible, she implores him to weigh everything carefully and to give his positive determination afterward. On the one side is the good being done to so many souls and renewed friendship and amity between the Wesleys and their neighbors; and on the other, the malicious objections of a few. Not content to leave it there, she adds that there will be terrible consequences if the meetings are stopped. It will cause ill will among the parishioners, and contrary to what Inman may hope or think, his known opposition to it will cause many to be angry with him and to avoid church altogether. Her closing comments are an adept summing up of the situation, cleverly laying the onus firmly upon Samuel:

> If you do after all think fit to dissolve this assembly, do not tell me any more that you desire me to do it, for that will not satisfy my conscience, but send me your positive command in such full and express terms as may absolve me from all guilt and punishment for neglecting this opportunity of doing good to souls, when you and I shall appear before the great and awful tribunal of our Lord Jesus Christ.
>
> I dare not wish this practice of ours had never been begun, but it will be with extreme grief that I shall dismiss

them, because I foresee the consequences. I pray God direct and bless you.[120]

Her combination of reasonable arguments about the positive effects of the prayer meetings and her appeal to Samuel's own sense of the necessity of doing good for the souls of his parishioners in his absence caused him to rethink his position. Samuel wisely backed down, allowing the meetings to continue until his return from London.[121] Yet again, Susanna found ways of living out her faith and attending to her own freedom of conscience within the tightly structured society of which she was a part by submitting to the subordinate role in which she was placed by birth but deftly exalting her vocation as a Christian under the authority of God.

The experience of her worship leadership and her passionate defense of her little society surely made a lasting impression as John Wesley later employed similar types of Christian Conferencing between people banded together into little societies for spiritual formation and growth and as he was confronted by other extraordinary women called to witness to the gospel using unorthodox methods.[122] Her insistence on the liberty of one's God-guided conscience in the face of human opposition influenced his later defense of Methodist breaches of Church of England convention and also informed his astonishing advice to Sophy Hopkey after her marriage to William Williamson that she should obey God rather than her husband when her husband's will was contrary to God's.[123] Susanna Wesley's fingerprints can be clearly discerned throughout Methodism; she is rightfully regarded as the "devotional, theological, and ecclesiastical mother of the Methodist revival."[124]

"I Do Indeed Rejoice in My Sons"

Keeping a personal spiritual diary, educating her children, creating essays for her children's religious instruction, and providing spiritual advice by writing letters were not unusual activities for a woman of Susanna's day, but leading public worship and writing a published controversial tract certainly were. When theological differences over predestination led to a break between her sons and George White-field, a longtime friend of both John and Charles Wesley, Susanna took pen in hand for an anonymous rebuttal of Whitefield's position and a defense of John Wesley's theological position. Though she was critical of some aspects of the Methodist revival, this remark-able document reveals the depth of her support as she turns her considerable theological acumen toward the debate.

Upon the publication of John Wesley's sermon "Free Grace" and Whitefield's spirited Calvinist response, a pamphlet entitled "Some Remarks on a Letter from the Reverend Mr Whitefield to the Reverend Mr Wesley, in a Letter from a Gentlewoman to Her Friend" was printed anonymously, though all the evidence both internal and external points to Susanna as its author.[125] Her author-ship was suspected at the time of publication but not conclusively proven until the 1960s by Frank Baker who considered it a com-petent apologia for Methodism, though "perhaps not as impressive as some other examples of Mrs. Wesley's work."[126] Charles Wal-lace likewise agrees that it is not particularly sophisticated theol-ogy but praises it as practical and possessing a rhetorical flare that illuminates the multifaceted aspects of the growing rift between John Wesley and George Whitefield, starting that it deserves seri-ous consideration as Susanna's last and most public proclamation of her theological convictions.[127]

Unimpressed by Whitefield's hasty and haphazard style of writ-ing, Susanna criticizes his habit of referring to John Wesley as "Dear" and "Honoured," calling them meaningless words that might signal Whitefield's intent to "cut his friend's throat with a feather."[128] She sharply asserts that Whitefield is "beating the air, sometimes arguing against self-evident truth" and at other times "against the truth of God himself." She is quick to note that the larger provocation in the quarrel is the Wesleyan emphasis on "gospel holiness" rather than their "pleading so strongly for universal redemption, and if they [the Wesleys] would let the former alone, they [the Calvinists] would forgive them the latter."[129] She closes by observing that God has honored these two brothers by calling and enabling them to preach the gospel and by putting a seal to their ministry, and she asks that her reader will hold them in prayer so that God will continue to strengthen and protect them, to keep them steadfast and faithful in their labors.

The depth of Susanna's approval cannot simply be attributed to her position as the mother of John and Charles Wesley; this is, after all, a woman who had followed her own conscience in opposition to her closest male relatives since her youth. She did not hesitate to disagree if warranted, and she had been instrumental in leading John to overcome his initial reluctance to lay preaching when he learned that Thomas Maxfield, a layman, had done so in the absence of clergy at a society meeting.[130] The immensity of her encouragement of this act and the vital influence it had on the nature of Methodism can hardly be overstated. Because of her, John Wesley began to see the possibilities in lay preaching and began to utilize it as a primary means for spreading the gospel since he did not have enough clergymen to do so. In due time, this initial step of authorizing some laymen to preach led to his endorsement of the exhorting and even preaching of women he judged to have an extraordinary call.

Her approbation of the work and theology of her sons is evident also in a personal letter written to Lady Huntingdon in July 1741 in which she expresses gratitude for Lady Huntingdon's kindness. She glows with affection and rejoices in their unconventional ministry, caring little what others may think about them because of her conviction that it is pleasing to God:

> I do indeed rejoice in my sons and am much pleased, that they have in any measure been serviceable to your ladyship. You'll pardon the fondness of a mother, if I exceed in commending them, but I've known few (if any) that have laboured more diligently and unweariedly in the service of our dear Lord. And, blessed be his great name, he hath set his seal to their ministry and hath made them instrumental in bringing many souls to God. And though in the eye of the world they appear despicable, men of no estate or figure, and daily suffer contempt, reproach and shame among

men, yet to me they appear more honourable than they would do if the one were Archbishop of Canterbury and the other of York; for I esteem the reproach of Christ greater riches than all the treasures in England.[131]

A letter to Charles also expresses her admiration for John's zeal, particularly when it is tempered with "meekness and patience and longsuffering" and when his opposition to the Calvinist doctrine of predestination is flavored with a "true spirit of Christian charity." She exhibits a sense of fulfillment that her life's work is bearing great fruit in the lives and ministry of her sons, declaring that she can see the power of God manifest in the Methodist revival. All her life, she had labored to educate all her children in the things of God, and Charles and John are marvelously employed in that same work, being renewed in strength day by day.[132]

"A Wise Counsellor . . . and a Sound Spiritual Director"

Susanna Wesley's piety, her devotion to prayer and meditation through her spiritual journal, her unwavering commitment to educating her family in the things of God, her willingness to step out of customary gender roles in order to lead, and her burning desire to love and serve God with her intellect and her entire life continue to inspire us today. She was uniquely gifted and well-equipped for her role in encouraging the Methodist revival by example and by precept. As Adam Clarke admiringly wrote of her, "The good sense, piety, observation, and experience, of Mrs. Wesley, qualified her to be a wise counsellor in almost every affair in life, and a sound spiritual director in most things that concerned the salvation of the soul."[133]

Susanna Wesley was both a traditional woman of her time *and* an extraordinary woman who frequently stepped across the accepted boundaries of feminine behavior while still claiming adherence to those same conventions, based upon her trust in an authority higher than her husband or her church. Her deep devotion, intellectual powers, and educational grounding combined with a strong will and independence of thought formed her into a formidable thinker and writer as well as a well-equipped spiritual guide and pastor to her family and community. In some ways aided and in others limited by the religious establishment and wider societal expectations of a woman's role, she takes her place as a foundational "Mother of Israel" among the people called Methodists, whose legacy lives on in the stories of other early Methodist women and in the ministries of her spiritual descendants today.

TWO

An Overview of Women's Roles in Early Methodism

The Backbone of Early Methodism

Although women like Sarah Ryan, Sarah Crosby, Mary Bosanquet Fletcher, and Hester Ann Roe Rogers were close friends of John Wesley and their ministries were held in high regard by him and other early Methodists, most potential United Methodist ministers escape from seminary having read little about them or their sisters in faith. However, their writings have long been highly influential in the spiritual journeys and ministries of many Wesleyan Holiness women as they discerned a call beyond the domestic sphere. Fletcher and Rogers in particular were prolific writers of letters, journals, and spiritual autobiographies, and many of their books remained in print during the nineteenth century on both sides of the Atlantic.[1]

Susanna Wesley's ministry began with her role as "pious mother" and almost accidentally developed into "public preacher," a pattern repeated in the experience of some women preachers.[2] Examining their own words and the testimony of those who knew them reveals many of the same spiritual qualities seen in Susanna Wesley: deep piety, devotion to prayer, liberty of conscience, and a burning desire to love, serve, and proclaim the gospel regardless of opposition and even danger. John Wesley recognized these characteristics and created or allowed spaces for their voices to be heard and for their ministries to flourish. He helped ordinary people, laymen and laywomen, to examine, value, and account for their own spiritual experience and to trust the inner witness of the Spirit.[3]

There were signs in his early ministry that John Wesley appreciated the gifts of women in varying roles in the church. Influenced by the Moravians while in Georgia, he instituted many innovations in religious practice that became characteristic of the Methodist revival: lay leaders, extemporaneous preaching and prayer, and in a revival of ancient practices of the Church, he appointed deaconesses whose "office" was to visit the sick and instruct other women in private but not to teach publicly. He appointed at least three women for these tasks: Margaret Burnside, Mrs. Gilbert, and Mary Vanderplank.[4]

Moravian women held a variety of leadership positions within their "choirs," which were divided according to sex, marital status, and age, an idea Wesley adapted in the development of Methodist classes and bands.[5] Later, upon his return to England in 1738, he continued to value women's gifts. As theological differences began to fragment the Fetter Lane Society and attempts were made to exclude women from some activities, he indignantly wrote to the Moravian leaders: "I do exceedingly disapprove of the excluding of women when we meet to pray, sing, and read the Scriptures."[6]

Methodism prized individual experience, which gave women greater latitude in the expression of their religious lives. This nurture of piety was an area where women could find meaning outside the domestic sphere as well as within, leading many of the more educated among them to write, publish, and act in ways that transcended the limits placed on them. Good women were supposed to keep silent, but many found that their duty to God or to their children compelled them to speak.[7] Within the framework of Methodist bands and societies, they felt free to use their gifts for prayer, testimony, exhorting, and eventually expounding and preaching. This challenge to the accepted gender order led to accusations from those hostile to the revival that Methodism disrupted family life and even that it encouraged sexual license because of their lengthy meetings that included women and men, especially the love feasts. There were even riots in Wednesbury and Chester triggered by these charges of neglect of domestic life.[8]

Methodism nurtured community in its gatherings, providing fresh ways of making friends and even for creating replacements for family, as in the lives of Mary Bosanquet and her companions, Sarah Ryan, Sarah Lawrence, Sarah Crosby, and others. In the narratives of many of these women, it is clear that in becoming Methodists, they were in effect renouncing dominant eighteenth-century British culture by declaring their allegiance to their new spiritual family, and time and again, they proved that they were willing to give up nearly everything in the process.

This liberty of conscience and self-determination, despite opposition, criticism, and ostracism, is a defining feature in the lives of many women who joined the Methodists. Like Susanna Wesley before them, these women acted in these ways not to make a feminist statement or to foment revolution but because their commitment and obedience were to a much higher authority than mainstream culture.[9] As they engaged in ministries typically regarded as lying outside the realm of appropriate feminine behavior and as they faced criticism for those ministries, they justified their activities through their letters, journals, and other writings, along with the fruit borne of their efforts, and by appealing to John Wesley for sanction.

John Wesley and Women of Early Methodism

It is of course impossible to speak of these early Methodist women without drawing on their relationships with other Methodist women and men, as well as, of course, their relationship with John Wesley himself. Moving skillfully between the private and public spheres, women like Mary Bosanquet Fletcher and Sarah Crosby frequently tested the boundaries of acceptable female behavior, understanding themselves to be answering a call from God not only to feed the sheep but also to make known publicly what God had done for their souls. Their ministries were sustained by mutual spiritual mentoring and with the counsel of their "Father" in Christ, John Wesley.[10]

While Wesley's romantic relationships with women, including his marriage, were dismal failures, his closest friends and spiritual advisors (other than his brother Charles) were women.[11] Theirs was a letter-writing age, and Wesley was a master of the genre, utilizing frequent epistles to provide spiritual guidance, pastoral care, reproof, and correction. He wrote to other religious leaders and ordained clergy, to new converts and lay preachers, and to ordinary Methodists alike, notably sharing his emotions more readily with women than with men. With men he was affectionate, practical, and critical, even sarcastic. With women his tone might be pleading, confiding, or questioning, but most often he wrote to them as a mentor, a counselor, and a friend.[12] Methodism's emphasis on personal religious experience found profound expression among women as they appeared more open to freely addressing matters of the heart, and Wesley encouraged them to share their thoughts freely in their letters to him, in their personal journals, and in public testimony.

Over the years, women from various walks of life were the recipients of a large number of John Wesley's epistles. The letters addressed a gamut of concerns. He asked about their spiritual lives, offered medical advice, advised, encouraged, and challenged them, urged them to go on to perfection, and directed their reading and devotional studies. No aspect of life was beyond his interest and pastoral guidance. Importantly, the sheer volume of letters written by Wesley to women

> serves to emphasize the way in which Wesley was sensitive to the feminine mystique, appreciated feminine achievements, and encouraged the leadership of women in his societies. Clearly they were not all fashioned from the same mould. . . . They shared some important characteristics, however, which drew and retained Wesley's interest: they evinced a strong dedication to personal spirituality, and were usually strongly allied to the Methodist societies; they engaged as far as their health allowed in practical religious service; they were thoughtful and intelligent. Most of them were also teachable and deferential, perhaps partly because

they were younger—and toward the end of the list, considerably younger—than Wesley himself. It should be said, however, that although Wesley in his seventies and eighties undoubtedly warmed to the company and correspondence of attractive young female disciples, he would brush them off if they proved to be empty-headed hero-worshippers.[13]

John Wesley was in many ways a walking paradox. He was undoubtedly authoritarian and patriarchal to the core, tightly holding on to control of many aspects of the Methodist revival, and yet he made room for women's voices to be heard through their spiritual autobiographies and their letters, as well as through their public speaking and preaching. Crucially, rather than isolating or setting them against each other, Wesley promoted friendship among them and sought to help them connect with each other for mutual support and friendship.[14]

The Importance of Female Friendship in Early Methodism

John Wesley often linked a more mature Christian woman with a newly justified or sanctified woman. For example, in a letter written June 3, 1774, to Sarah Crosby, usually regarded as the first of the female Methodist preachers, Wesley asks her to "tenderly and carefully" watch over young Elizabeth Ritchie lest she fall prey to temptations that might move her from her steadfastness. In the same letter, perhaps referring to an earlier disagreement between Sarah Crosby and Mary Bosanquet, he rejoices that the two are now communicating more freely than before, warning Crosby to guard against the devices of Satan, who would gladly tear Elizabeth and her asunder. Because of his trust in her and his high regard for her spiritual maturity, he also asks Sarah Crosby in a letter of June 3, 1774, to counsel one of the itinerant *men*, a former soldier named Duncan Wright, fearing that he had "suffered loss" in his ministry.[15]

Similarly, on June 23, 1774, he writes to Elizabeth Ritchie that Satan "neither slumbers nor sleeps, and he will strive to torment if he cannot destroy." Urging her "to fight the good fight of faith and thus to lay hold on eternal life," he notes that this requires believers to "keep close together, to walk hand in hand, and provoke one another to love and to good works."[16] Two years later, on November 12, 1776, a concerned Wesley praises Elizabeth Ritchie for her frankness in her letters to him, telling her: "At all times it is of use to have a friend to whom you can pour out your heart without any disguise or reserve. But it will be of peculiar use if you should ever meet with heavy temptation. Then you will find how true that word is, 'A friend is made for adversity.' "[17]

Wesley encouraged women to develop and use their gifts, sympathized with their struggles, and directed their devotional and theological reading and their prayer lives. His boundless energy and undoubted leadership skills enabled him to identify with people of different educational backgrounds, economic status, and intellectual abilities; and his affinity for friendship with women offered him a space in which to unburden himself, to seek spiritual counsel, and to relate his own need for support and prayer in ways he could not freely do with other men. Throughout his long life, Wesley saw in women a "capacity for an ardent spirituality that aroused both his curiosity and his humble admiration."[18]

While male preachers itinerated and had less opportunity to form or strengthen bonds because of their constant traveling, Methodist women lived in more stable environments and communities where regular class and band meetings inculcated religious conversation and mutual confession and support.[19] Women were the backbone of the Methodist revival, making up a considerable proportion of society members. In April 1742, for example, in Wesley's list of the sixty-six leaders in the Foundry Society, forty-two were women.[20] They participated publicly in a wide range of controversial activities and leadership practices, which evolved as they experienced God's call to various types of service, although preaching was a later development only slowly accepted and encouraged by John Wesley. It was sometimes said that the early Methodist societies were in fact "organizations of women."[21] For many women, the intimacy of Christian friendships and fellowship experienced

42

in band and class meetings was an important means of grace that sustained them as they cared for the sick and poor and grew in love and grace together.

In addition to attending Methodist worship and leading classes and bands, Methodist women hosted traveling preachers and devoted themselves to acts of charity and mercy like visiting back-sliders and prisoners. Many became intimate spiritual friends and advisors of male preachers, including John and Charles Wesley, and they nurtured strong bonds of spiritual kinship with other women, often living communally. They founded schools and orphanages and nursed the sick. Some married itinerant preachers and exercised their ministry in that role, while many others remained single or were widowed.[22]

Prayer groups were organized and led by women, and when there were no clergy readily available in their communities, women started new societies and eventually rose to leadership in the classes, which were obligatory, while the more spiritually mature also led bands. Wealthy women like the Countess of Huntingdon also committed financial resources to build preaching houses and chapels. While John Wesley liked to exert a certain amount of control over their activities, he also encouraged them to use their God-given talents and to share their experience of God with others through both the written and spoken word. Such public speaking and letter writing gave women social, psychological, and spiritual space in which to exercise spiritual agency and authority during a time in which those opportunities were scarce.

The classes and bands that formed the structure of Wesleyan Methodism coupled with Wesley's encouragement of women to join each other to form Christian bonds for mutual support enabled the formation of female friendships and even literal households or communities. These were crucially important for the development of women's public proclamation and for enlarging the sphere in which women exercised spiritual leadership.

This web of female friendships often cut across economic and social status, as seen in the sisterhood between Sarah Ryan, a former domestic servant with a "past" who was the onetime housekeeper at the New Room in Bristol, and Mary Bosanquet, the educated daughter of a well-to-do tradesman.[23] Because Mary Bosanquet was so much superior socially to Sarah Ryan, their relationship naturally drew criticism. Some of Mary's friends wondered why she did not choose a companion who could contribute financially to the cost of setting up a school and orphanage at Leytonstone.[24] Her response was eloquent, denying the importance of financial or social gain in relationships. Instead she extolled the virtue of true friendship and the joy of being united with such a spiritual helper as Sarah Ryan, thereby rejecting the typical qualities prized by men in their relationships with women: wealth, social standing, comfort, and sexual gratification, instead substituting friendship.[25]

In Leytonstone in 1763, with Sarah Ryan's assistance, Mary Bosanquet established a household that provided education and housing for orphaned children. This household also became a center for Methodist women's activity and community.[26] Over many years, Sarah Crosby, Sarah Lawrence, Mary Tooth, and many others visited or lived together there or at Cross Hall in Yorkshire, drawing spiritual strength and encouragement from each other as they shared the work of ministry and validated each other's spiritual experience. These women of the Fletcher circle were a gathered community connected by something other than the inherited ties of class and family; they were in a sense Methodism in microcosm, a family based not on biology but on shared spirituality.[27]

The boundaries between the public and private spheres were constantly expanding and contracting and sometimes blending as Methodist women moved between the two. The "private space of family and friendship often merged seamlessly with public space of neighborhood, community, religious society, class, and congregation, and private letters sometimes became rhetorical public documents."[28] Such writings were used by Wesley as a means to transmit Methodist theology and to form the religious identities of the reader.

Women's Writings: Private and Public

Even journals, which one might consider the most private of documents, were written with one eye toward potential readers, as Wesley himself published "extracts" from his own journal in installments from 1739 to 1791 and encouraged Methodist women and men to share theirs with him and by extension with the world, particularly by being published in the *Arminian Magazine*. Wesley's intent was to produce tracts on the universal love of God and God's willingness to save all people from all sin. He provided examples from the spiritual autobiographies of holy women and men and published their letters and accounts of their religious experience, as well as inspirational poetry.[29]

Life writings published in the *Arminian* were strictly regulated by Wesley, who expected them to conform to a particular pattern that would inspire others to lives of holiness. Wesley solicited, selected, and edited only the most exemplary lives and spiritual journals of pious women and men. The magazine was not explicit about the ministry practices of female preachers, but Wesley reprinted letters from Mary Bosanquet, Sarah Crosby, Elizabeth Ritchie, and others, in which they reported on their evangelistic efforts, including preaching.[30] He was their strongest ally, and upon his death, there was no immediate successor to champion their cause. Significantly, such published accounts also included the writings of non-preaching "rank and file" women and men.

Realizing that many were not well-educated and might be anxious about the quality of their writing, John Wesley offered to edit their letters before publication.[31] He published the journal of a woman named Elizabeth Harper, praising it as the simple account of an average woman who was writing for her own use. Her journal contains reminders of religious conversations, her thoughts and interpretations of various scripture passages, confessions of her temptations, lists of her prayers and blessings, and details of her method of praying for the members of her band, providing a rich resource for ordinary readers to identify with and use as a pattern for their own reflective journals.[32]

In the preface to the published volume of her journal, Wesley approvingly wrote: "I have no doubt, but God had all her heart." By making her experience widely available, he provided a model of journal-keeping that anyone might identify with and follow, and with his own published journals, he constructed a paradigm for how ordinary Methodists might read and write their own lives.[33] It is not hard to see how this solicitation and distribution of such highly personal spiritual material provided a certain freedom of expression for women that challenged the normal order of the day.

Women of early Methodism, like their sisters in other religious traditions, wrote to inspire faith, to support and educate, to encourage and challenge, and to offer reminders of God's grace for those who were suffering. They exchanged letters with each other, shared their religious journals, and sprinkled written and oral conversation with quotes from hymns by Charles Wesley and others. In doing so, they preserved the ties that bound them together in Christian love and influenced the shape of developing Methodist societies and classes.

Societies, Classes, and Bands

Methodism's structure itself provided spaces in which women began to more freely testify to their own experiences of justifying, saving, and even perfecting grace. The initial "unit" of Methodism was called a "society." Such a designation was not unique to Methodism, as the Church of England had various societies, including the Society for the Propagation of the Gospel, under whose auspices John Wesley had traveled to Georgia, and the Moravian Fetter Lane Society, in which the Wesleys had also participated.

A Methodist society consisted of a congregation of men and women who had been "awakened" by the Wesleys, George Whitefield, or other Methodist preachers. These itinerant preachers included laymen, a departure from the Anglican tradition that linked ordination as a priest with the role of preaching. Wesley held both a functional and an ecclesiastical view of pastors, distinguishing between "priests" (the church's *ordinary* ministers) and "prophets" (*extraordinary* ministers). As an ordained clergyman himself who was anxious that Methodism remain within the Church of England, he upheld the ecclesiastical authority of ordained priests and urged Methodists to attend their parish churches regularly and to receive the sacrament there. Because he realized that not all clergy were intent on nurturing the spiritual growth and holiness of their flocks, he utilized his itinerant preachers and class leaders to act as spiritual guides, thereby functioning as pastors to the people of the societies.[34]

Wesley himself traced the beginnings of the United Societies to late 1739 when several people who felt convinced of their sin and who were "groaning for redemption" approached him in London to request that he pray with them and advise them how to flee from the wrath to come. They decided to meet each week on Thursday evening, and their number grew quickly. At these gatherings, Wesley listened to them, prayed with them, and gave them spiritual counsel, and thus the United Society began in Methodism.

Wesley defined a society as "a company of men having the form and seeking the power of godliness, united in order to pray together, to receive the word of exhortation, and to watch over one another in love, that they may help each other to work out their salvation." In this way, the United Societies began, first in London and then in Bristol, Newcastle, and other places; and by 1743, Wesley had codified the expectations and rules for membership. Entrance to a society required only that one declare "a desire to flee from the wrath to come, to be saved from their sins," but for those in classes and bands, adherence to the General Rules of the United Societies was essential: (1) to avoid harm, (2) do good, and (3) attend upon the ordinances of God, the means of grace.[35] Members were then divided up into classes, grouped together by geography, and bands. Methodist bands were composed of "five to ten persons who agreed to meet regularly for intense spiritual nurture and support. Their primary activities were confession and prayer; their goal was spiritual growth."[36]

Since Wesley saw the movement as a revival within the Church of England and not as a precursor to the creation of a new church, he encouraged regular attendance at Methodist preaching services and society meetings but consistently required Methodists to continue worshiping at their parish churches. Here they would receive Communion, attend morning prayer, have their children baptized, marry, and be buried. Within the societies, they would hear Methodist preaching and exhorting and gather with others for mutual support and encouragement through worship and hymn singing. As a person grew in faith, she or he would then be invited to join a band and a class in which members discussed their spiritual experiences with each other and received more individual spiritual nurture and accountability.[37]

The role of these classes and bands in early Methodism became crucial as the revival spread and numbers increased. Bands, composed of like-minded individuals, were designed for intense spiritual sharing and growth manifest in confessing sins and self-examination. Like the Moravian choirs, these groups were single sex and composed of people sharing the same marital status. With a more rigorous discipline, bands became the place where more experienced believers met for encouragement while classes included newly awakened individuals as well as more seasoned members.

The desire to liquidate the debt on the New Room in Bristol had led to the creation of the class. At the suggestion of one of Wesley's emerging leaders, a Captain Foy, it was decided that these groups of ten or twelve people would meet for spiritual growth each week and bring a penny a week to pay off the building. The leaders were responsible for making up any shortage since some members were too poor to contribute. Ever practical, Wesley saw this as an excellent way to manage the debt while cultivating growth in holiness and providing close pastoral oversight since he could not meet individually with the rapidly growing number of Methodists.

Classes provided discipline for everyone in a society, while bands were for the more spiritually mature. Classes became the basic unit of Methodism, and they might be single sex or composed of both women and men. Larger than bands, classes were the locus for giving testimonies, sharing conversion stories, receiving instruction, and lovingly correcting each other in mutual accountability. Members were expected to give voice to their struggles and triumphs in their pilgrimage of faith and to speak freely about their souls. Class and band leaders would share candidly about their battles with temptation and sin as well as their growth in grace and sanctification.

These classes and bands were the foundational structure of Methodism, providing a safe place for discipline, fellowship, and identification.[38] These gatherings inculcated and nourished the public speaking of women and opened leadership roles to women in ways the Church of England had never permitted; their position in the Established Church allowed only for a backstage role in which they prayed, worshiped, gave alms, nursed the sick, and supported the male clergy.

In contrast, women who served as class and band leaders were not passive consumers of religion; they were trained, spiritually mature, servant ministers who cared for each other in mutual love.[39] They supervised meetings, visited the sick and backsliders, gave spiritual counsel, and prayed with their members. Leaders were always trustworthy laity who were known well and respected by Wesley, who handpicked them for the position, having first examined them for evidence that they had experienced God's saving grace and were earnestly seeking holiness or Christian perfection.[40]

Generally, women served as leaders over other groups of women, while men (other than preachers) rarely led exclusively female classes, but occasionally a woman might lead a mixed class. A woman might earn the title "Mother in Israel" by demonstrating her own piety through actively cultivating the faith of the members of her class. Dorothy Downes, a frequent correspondent of Wesley, wrote to ask his views on the propriety of a woman meeting with a male class. He replied: "As to the question you propose, if the leader himself desires it and the class be not unwilling, in that case there can be no objection to your meeting a class even of men. This is not properly assuming or exercising any authority over them. You do not act as a superior, but an equal; and it is an act of friendship and brotherly love."[41]

After weathering many initial threats from mobs and criticism from disapproving clergy, Wesley's system of organization was pretty well in place by the middle of the 1740s. He was, of course, at the top along with a small group of sympathetic Anglican clergy, including Charles Wesley; below them and supervised closely by Wesley were the lay preachers called "helpers" or "assistants." They were committed to the supervision of societies and the spread of Methodism as itinerant preachers. The third and largest group included local, non-itinerating preachers, stewards, housekeepers, leaders of the bands and classes, and visitors of the sick. The offices of band and class leader, housekeeper, and sick visitor were the chief areas in which women found the greatest opportunity to lead; and at least one Methodist woman, Mary Gilbert, performed the service of a steward even if not formally acknowledged as such.[42]

The Office of Housekeeper

The role of housekeeper was of greater significance than might first be obvious, as it was an office within the developing Methodist structure. Housekeeping among the Methodists called for a high level of maturity in faith, the exercise of spiritual responsibilities for a large household, and excellent management abilities in the execution of those duties. Naturally, housekeepers carried out a ministry of hospitality and were responsible for overseeing the care and well-being of any guests or residents in the Methodist preaching houses and for providing for their temporal needs. Even more importantly, they exercised considerable spiritual leadership as they were tasked with the overall supervision of the devotional practices and discipleship of those within their care. Offering Bible study, leading worship, and organizing the devotional life of the household by prayerful example, Methodist housekeepers in Bristol, London, and New-castle shouldered great responsibilities in their vocation of watching over their "families" in love.

Sarah Ryan

Because of her complicated marital history prior to her conversion, Wesley's appointment of Sarah Ryan in 1757 as housekeeper at the New Room in Bristol proved controversial and unpopular with some, including his wife Molly. But Wesley believed that God was clearly at work through and in her.[43] In 1779 in the *Arminian Magazine*, he printed her candid account of her life and religious experience as an example for others. She wrote that she was raised by devout parents and that she had occasionally felt the presence of God during the turbulent days before her conversion. Accompanying a friend to hear John Wesley preach at the Foundry, she had a remarkable spiritual experience during which she received a vision of Jesus standing before her as he had stood before Thomas, saying, "Reach hither thy hand, and thrust it into my side." She recorded that her heart melted, and she felt a strong desire to be united with the Methodists, but her inklings of faith melted away until she later met Sarah Crosby, one of the most respected women leaders and preachers among the Methodists.[44]

Lovingly held spiritually accountable by Sarah Crosby, Sarah Ryan became active in the society and class meetings and attended faithfully upon the means of grace, experiencing Holy Communion as a "converting sacrament" and eventually receiving the gift of sanctification. Perceiving a vision of Jesus and a little child standing together, she understood that she was the child but that she was being called to "grow up to the measure of his full stature," and she joyfully consecrated herself to Christ, willing to suffer and to sacrifice herself to work for his glory. She recorded that she "came home full of light, joy, love, and holiness; and God daily confirmed what he had done for my soul. And, blessed be his name. I now know where my strength lieth, and my soul is continually sinking more and more into God."[45] Accordingly, when John Wesley appointed her as housekeeper at the New Room, she accepted, recognizing this as a call to an important ministry.

In a letter to her dated November 8, 1757, Wesley lists the rules of the "family," which she is to observe in her post as housekeeper. These include regular hours of rising, going to bed, eating meals, praying together, and fasting. He instructs her to keep a strict watch over the conversation of visitors and members of the household so that the little community will be an example of holiness, and he reminds her that she is in a place of importance that will be closely observed and judged in the eyes of the world, by friends and enemies alike.

Realizing that she is neither well-educated nor experienced in leadership and that she is only recently converted to following the ways of God, Wesley encourages her to rely upon God's love and power to preserve her. He concludes, "Show that nothing is too hard for Him. Take to thee the whole armor of God and do and suffer all things through Christ strengthening thee. If you continue teachable and advisable, I know nothing that shalt be able to hurt you."[46]

Just as he freely offered guidance and spiritual direction in his letters to her, Wesley remarkably also felt free to express himself to her as a seeker and not just as the leader of the revival, seeing her as a spiritual friend in whom he could confide. In a letter of January 20, 1758, he writes to her: "The conversing with you . . . is an unspeakable blessing to me. I cannot think of you without thinking of God. Others often lead me to him, but it is, as it were, going round about: you bring me straight into his presence."[47] Wesley often wrote to her and other trusted women, asking for their prayers for him because he perceived that their religious ardor was greater than his and that they felt more deeply than he himself did.[48]

Having felt the love of God in a powerful way and having experienced strong spiritual renewal, despite her ill health and other obstacles, Sarah Ryan went on to live an exemplary life as one of Methodism's earliest female exhorters. By the time of her death at age forty-four, she was so highly regarded that she was remembered as a Mother in Israel, due largely to her influence on Methodism at large through her writings and especially through the work of her "daughters" in Christ.

Sarah Perrin

Sarah Ryan was not the first to hold the key position of housekeeper at the New Room. Sarah Perrin, a Quaker woman, preceded her in 1744, and like Sarah Ryan and Grace Murray (the house-keeper at the orphanage in Newcastle) she, too, became an early female Methodist exhorter. Attracted to Methodism and intrigued by its emphasis on individual and social renewal, she felt a tension between this new movement and her own Quaker background. She had apparently already been engaged in conversation with Charles Wesley for some time prior to writing a letter to him in December 1740 in which she describes the current state of her soul and the effect the Methodist revival was having on her:

> I have considered our last conversation and I have desired to partake of the same Christian courage which I rejoice to behold in you, O may I learn to speak the truth with bold-ness, nay I have thought I should be willing to have less of the divine sweetness if it would please my master to give me in exchange the gift of edifying others.[49]

The combination of her Quaker upbringing with its emphasis on the freedom of women to testify and her ongoing experiences of Methodism enabled her to courageously edify others by speaking of the things of God in public. A letter to Charles Wesley in 1741 contains a report of her experience (as a Quaker, no less) with an *Anglican* group at Leominster in Herefordshire:

> Here seems to be some good stirring. Many of the Church of England meet often together to talk of things of God. They invited me to come amongst them. I have been with them several times, they seem to be united in spirit to me. I earnestly desire I may lay no stumbling block in their way but that the master . . . may give me words for their edifi-cation. I have no party to promote but love unfeigned, no doctrine to set up but faith in our Lord Jesus, and no reli-gion to press them to but holiness of heart. One evening I gave them the Sermon on Salvation by Faith, they much approved of it. I read the hymn to them let the mind be in you which was also in Christ, they said it comforted them,

and some of Sukey's [Susanna] Designe's letters to me I
believe has been of service.[50]

Grace Murray

Grace Murray, who became the housekeeper at the orphanage in
Newcastle in 1743, was another woman whose many gifts were
recognized by Wesley, and she began in London as a leader of a
band at the Foundry in 1742. In addition to her oversight of the
household and orphanage in Newcastle, she became a class leader
with one hundred people in two classes and was a leader of bands,
meeting one every day of the week. Her ministry included visitation
of the sick and backsliders, meeting with the Societies outside Newcastle, serving as a companion to Wesley as he traveled in Ireland,
exhorting and preaching. Perhaps not surprisingly, Grace Murray's
gifts for ministry, her life of piety and service, her zeal for the gospel, and her industry so impressed Wesley that he wanted to marry
her. Unfortunately, it was not to be, but it is tantalizing to imagine
how differently Methodism might have developed if Wesley had
partnered with a woman of her talents and devotion; alas, he and
the woman he did later marry, Molly Vazeille, were wildly unsuited.[51]

Visitor to the Sick

Wesley held a holistic understanding of salvation that considered
both spiritual and physical health important, and in his 1742 pamphlet "Character of a Methodist," he elaborates on this definition
of salvation:

> By salvation [the Methodist] means holiness of heart and
> life . . . a Methodist is one who has "the love of God shed
> abroad in his heart by the Holy Ghost given to him"; one who
> "loves the Lord his God with all his heart, and with all his soul,
> and with all his mind, and with all his strength." . . . [and] this
> commandment is written in his heart, that "he who loveth
> God, loves his brother also." . . . His obedience is in pro-
> portion to his love, the source from whence it flows. And

therefore, loving God with all his heart, he serves him with all his strength. . . . Lastly, as he has time, he "does good unto all men"—unto neighbours, and strangers, friends, and enemies. And that in every possible kind; not only to their bodies, by "feeding the hungry, clothing the naked, visiting those that are sick or in prison," but much more does he labour to do good to their souls, . . . that they may have peace with God.[52]

Believing that maintaining or restoring good health required not only prayer and self-discipline, Wesley also prescribed care of the body by a variety of common-sense methods such as avoidance of caffeine, going to bed and rising early, and taking regular exercise. This interest in the total well-being of a person is reflected in his collection of simple remedies, *Primitive Physick*, in his concern over widespread alcoholism, care for the needy, and the establishment of orphanages and schools, as well as his implementation of appointed volunteers to regularly visit and care for the sick.

Wesley encouraged all Methodists, male and female, to visit the sick, and the role of visitor of the sick became an essential component of the religious vocation of many women. Like many other developments in Methodism, it evolved out of simple need into an important, recognized ministry. In a letter to his brother Charles, John Wesley describes the emergence of this important office at the Foundry in London, reporting that eight or ten people offered to regularly visit the sick.[53] Only upon reflection did Wesley draw a link between these assigned visitors and the role of the deacons and deaconnesses in Acts. In *A Plain Account of the People Called Methodists,* he outlined the responsibilities of the visitor to the sick, noting that the position arose out of necessity since the stewards were unable to visit as often as they would like.

Wesley's description of the work of a visitor to the sick is indicative of his interest in the health of the whole person, body and spirit. Visitors were expected to call on the sick in their particular district three times a week, inquiring into and giving advice regarding the state of their souls, and helping them in any way possible. Wesley instructed them to be plain and open in their dealings with the people they visited, to be patient and tender, to be as clean as possible in caring for a person's needs, and to not be overly sensitive or squeamish about performing necessary tasks for the sufferer.[54]

Wesley's fullest explication of the importance of visiting the sick, in which he especially urged women to participate, is in his sermon "On Visiting the Sick," written late in his ministry in 1786. Here he gives a broad definition of "the sick" to include not just those who are bedridden or those who are generally considered sick but also those in a state of affliction, whether of body or mind. He understands this to include people who are bad as well as good and persons who do not fear God as well as those who do, and he includes the visitation of the poor as concomitant with care for the sick.

In keeping with his understanding that acts of mercy as well as acts of piety are a means of grace, Wesley views visitation of the sick as a real means of grace, taking its place in the list along with feeding the hungry, clothing the naked, relieving the stranger, and visiting the imprisoned. In his discussion here of the parable of the sheep and the goats (Matthew 25:31-46), he strongly asserts that these acts of mercy are not just nice, optional things for a Christian to do whenever there is free time; they are in a real sense an essential part of walking as Christ walked.

Anticipating some resistance, he refutes the idea that this can be done at a distance. When he uses the word "visit," that is exactly what he means: a face-to-face encounter with another human being. Sending assistance is certainly a good thing, but it is different from actually being present with the person who is sick.

To the objection that sending a doctor will do much more good for the sick than going oneself, Wesley agrees that a physician can do more with regard to bodily health, but he argues that a Christian visitor can do more good for their souls. Besides, Wesley insists, even if it were possible that the doctor could do more good for someone's soul, this still would not excuse the Christian from going since by not going one misses that means of grace and loses another opportunity to thank God for her or his own health and strength.[55] Similarly, Wesley believed that visiting the poor is also an act of mercy that both inculcated humility and served as a means of grace.[56] Visiting others in need is a basic Christian duty, not a ministry reserved for the ordained. It is part and parcel of the structure of a Christian's life. Accordingly, he delivers a scathing denunciation of those who make a point of avoiding this duty to the sick and the poor:

> One great reason why the rich in general have so little sympathy for the poor is because they so seldom visit them. Hence it is that, according to the common observation, one part of the world does not know what the other suffers. Many of them do not know, because they do not care to know; they keep out of the way of knowing it—and then plead their voluntary ignorance as an excuse for their hardness of heart. . . . How did this come to pass? Why, he took good care to keep out of their way. And if he fell upon any of them unawares, "he passed over on the other side."[57]

Using an example that is almost certainly aimed primarily at Methodist *women* who have been shirking this important ministry, Wesley holds up the example of gentlewomen and even royalty of Paris who have made it their business to visit and care for the sick, even by dressing their sores and performing the most lowly of necessary tasks for them. Wesley declares that, rather than following the latest craze in French fashion, their example of service to the sick is a far better pattern for the English of any station or status to follow. He unbends far enough to suggest that if someone is too delicate to tend to these admittedly lowly physical needs, supplying spiritual needs is still within one's ability to do, and this is to be done personally, not by proxy.[58]

For Wesley, it is clear that visitation of the sick is not dependent on any particular characteristic of either the recipient or the visitor but rather on the grace of God. Christ expects it of those who seek to follow him, and in the visitation of the sick, God is glorified and neighbor comforted. Additionally, visiting provides a way of seeing Christ in the face of the needy neighbor, an act in which both the visitor and the sick person can experience God's presence and grace. Wesley underlines the necessity of depending on God's grace and power in serving the sick, emphasizing the need to pray for wisdom, humility, patience, and long-suffering in order to avoid becoming discouraged or angry at the response of the person who is ill. He realistically points out some of the negative outcomes, especially with regard to the spiritual state of the sick,

> Be not moved with the deep ignorance of some, the dull-ness, the amazing stupidity of others; marvel not at their peevishness or stubbornness, at their non-improvement after all the pains that you have taken; yea, at some of the turning back to perdition, and being worse than they were before. Still your record is with the Lord, and your reward with the Most High.[59]

Wesley advises beginning a visit by asking about the person's outward condition and discovering whether she or he has food, clothing, and fuel, as well as someone to take care of these physical needs, and whether the person is receiving proper medical advice. This is essential because Wesley fully expects that the visitor may have to fight on the invalid's behalf to see that assistance is avail-able, being humble enough to beg and use any personal influence for the sick person. After seeing to those immediate needs, a visitor is then to turn to the care of the person's soul with reminders of God's goodness and providence, encouraging repentance and con-version and praying for full salvation. This evangelistic component of visiting the sick is accompanied by a more educational one, that of teaching industry and cleanliness, quoting a "pious man" who stated that "cleanliness is next to godliness."

Wesley concludes the sermon by treating in more detail the question of who is responsible for visiting the sick in more detail. He is particularly concerned that those who possess many of the world's goods turn their hands to this ministry since they generally have free time to spend with the sick, and they are able to use their privileged position in society to do good to the souls and bodies of those less fortunate. Their acts of charity will be gratefully received by the sick, who will then be inclined to listen more reverently to the gospel message. He insists that everyone has an obligation to visit and that all have something to offer. The wealthy can share their resources, while others who are poor can give their prayers. Those who are old can offer their experience and wisdom, and the young bring their vitality and energy.

Wesley then addresses in more detail the question of whether or not women should be involved in this honorable service to the sick and poor. A deep conviction that women as well as men are created in the image of God and that women both old and young were specifically appointed for this ministry in the early church leads him to respond affirmatively and passionately.

> Undoubtedly they may; nay, they ought—it is meet, right, and their bounden duty. Herein there is no difference; "there is neither male nor female in Christ Jesus." Indeed it has long passed for a maxim with many, that "women are only to be seen, not heard." And accordingly many of them are brought up in such a manner as if they were only designed for agreeable playthings. But is this doing honour to the sex? Or is it a real kindness to them? No; it is the deepest unkindness; it is horrid cruelty; . . . And I know not how any woman of sense and spirit can submit to it. Let all you that have it in your power assert the right which the God of nature has given you. Yield not to that vile bondage any longer. You, as well as men, are rational creatures. You, like them, were made in the image of God; you are equally candidates for immortality; you too are called of God, as you have time, to "do good unto all men." Be "not disobedient to the heavenly calling." Whenever you have opportunity, do all the good you can, particularly to your poor, sick neighbour. And every one of you likewise "shall receive your own reward, according to your own labour."[60]

Accordingly, with Wesley's support and encouragement, the women who pursued this visitation ministry as an opportunity for service exercised leadership not only in their care of the sick and poor but also in organizing charitable enterprises, visiting those in prison, and engaging in various forms of public speaking within and beyond the class and band meetings.[61] Their activity among the sick presented them with numerous occasions for casual conversations about faith, for prayer, and in some circumstances, for exhortation. Apparently, this was a ministry at which Grace Murray excelled. Among her other responsibilities as housekeeper in Newcastle, she was a diligent visitor of the sick and a caring nurse who described visiting the sick as a "delight." She was apparently also a very effective visitor to backsliders, a role that she called "pleasant meat," and her reputation for being a fine exhorter meant that she had frequent invitations to speak and travel with Wesley and other Methodist preachers from time to time.[62]

As the women's field of service expanded to include visiting in prisons, personal testimony, scripture reading, and exhorting the unconverted, Wesley and his ordained colleagues gave their approval to the varied activities of these women.[63] The ministry of one woman, Sarah Peters, was especially fruitful, earning her accolades in the *Arminian Magazine* from Wesley: "it was her particular gift and her continual care, to seek and save that which was lost; to support the weak, to comfort the feeble-minded, to bring back what had been turned out of the way."[64] Sadly, her unflagging dedication to prayer, exhortation, and exposition of scripture among the prisoners, especially her unwearied efforts to comfort and convert those condemned to death, led to her untimely death of "prison fever."[65]

Nevertheless, women persisted in these ministries. That they did so despite the disapproval of their families and much of eighteenth-century society was an indication of their dedication to answer the divine call in obedience, whatever the cost. Their conviction of the rightness of such action in the face of societal disparagement also empowered them to conquer the anxiety that naturally accompanied such actions, especially as they embarked on ministries of publicly proclaiming the gospel.

The Trajectory of Women's Public Speaking

Earl Kent Brown has identified several modes of public expression used by early Methodist women, beginning with "the most informal to the most formal: (a) casual conversation among acquaintances; (b) speaking or praying in band and class meetings; (c) prayer in society and other public meetings; (d) testimony; (e) exhortation; (f) expounding; and (g) biblical exegesis and application."[66]

Methodism was conceived as a revival movement within the Church of England, and Wesley did not want to give the impression that he wanted to start a new church. He was anxious to avoid comparisons with Non-Conformists like the Quakers and Baptists, both of whom had women preachers, so he drew these careful distinctions in an attempt to deflect criticism of women acting in an "inappropriate" manner. However, the lines between these various expressions became blurred as time went by, and no matter how much he split hairs, it became apparent that some women were in fact preaching.[67]

Casual Conversation

Casual conversation hardly needs further explication, consisting of informal talking among friends on religious topics, especially those who were spiritual seekers. Any Methodist woman might be expected to participate in this practice. Such conversation might take place almost anywhere as women went about their normal daily activities, and it often consisted of one's own witness to the Spirit and an invitation to attend a Society meeting.

Speaking and Praying in Bands or Classes

Speaking or praying in bands or classes was the first opportunity many women had for speaking before a group. Women served as leaders in classes and bands, inviting discussion through catechesis or direct questions of the group, and publicly testifying about their own experience of God. Formal discussion might be accompanied by spiritual counsel and reproof for sin and sometimes included the "enforcing" of a particular text by noting parallels in other scriptures or in the tradition of the church.[68]

Praying at Society Meetings

Praying in the much larger society meetings offered women an even more public venue for speaking and was seen as an appropriate way for women to speak. One such woman, Ann Cutler, spent hours each day in lengthy private prayer and became known as "Praying Nanny." She felt that intercessory prayer was her particular call, and while her public prayers were shorter, they were apparently criticized by some as being too loud. Nevertheless, she continued.[69]

Testimony

Public testimony of one's personal religious experience was another common mode of utterance for Methodist women. This was a regular feature of the love feast, a practice rooted in scripture and modeled on the Moravians' example. Writing in his journal in an entry dated July 19, 1761, John Wesley approvingly writes: "I hastened back to the love-feast at Birstall. It was the first of the kind which had been there. Many were surprised when I told them, 'The very design of a love-feast is a free and familiar conversation, in which every man, yea, and woman has liberty to speak whatever may be to the glory of God.'"[70]

He did not consider such testifying to be preaching, but as in bands and classes, the love feasts and other public gatherings gave opportunities for women to express themselves with candor and openness. As they began to bear witness to their awakened faith, they ventured into areas traditionally confined to men and moved ever closer to what Wesley defined as preaching. The immediacy of testimony offered women direct access to their audience, and their obvious sincerity and persuasiveness created more acceptance of the practice.

Not surprisingly, many women were hesitant or nervous about speaking publicly, even though they felt they were acting in obedience to God's call and believed that failure to do so would imperil their own salvation. Sibyl Best spoke of her heart sinking within her when she received the impression of the Holy Spirit urging her to preach, but she became convinced that her call from God was no less clear than her call to conversion and that she must preach or perish.[71]

Exhortation

Exhortation was also regarded by Wesley as an acceptable form of public speaking for women that fell short of preaching because it consisted of pleas for sinners to hear the gospel message and respond to it, to repent and be saved. After the preacher finished his sermon, the exhorter would rise and urge the congregation to apply the words to their own lives, motivating them to repent and live a more Christian life, and worshipers became accustomed to seeing and hearing women in this role.[72] Exhorting did not include taking a text and speaking directly on scripture; instead, it was a brief address following the preaching of Wesley or one of the itinerants that was intended to reinforce what the people had already heard.[73]

Exhorting might also arise by necessity when a woman found herself in circumstances that called for a word from God to be shared with her listeners. Hester Ann Roe (later Rogers) prayed publicly and led classes. She also occasionally exhorted and felt compelled to do so during an earthquake that occurred in Macclesfield during a worship service. She records the fear of the congregation, some of whom shrieked, fainted, and called for God to have mercy on them. She remained calm and felt the Spirit nudge her to speak, with the result that many were converted as a result.

> But O, unspeakable grace. My heart was kept calm, for I feared not to die. That scripture was brought to my mind: "Yet once more, and I shake not the earth only, but also heaven." And I was able to exhort those around to be still, and look unto the God of grace for salvation, which they had too long neglected.[74]

Expounding

Expounding came much closer to actual preaching, as a woman might base her speaking upon scriptural themes or texts or perhaps upon some uplifting biography or article. This typically included Wesley's sermons or other writings of spiritual counsel, and for some, like Mary Bosanquet Fletcher, the expounding often took the form of catechetical question and answer, using one's own life experience or some "awakening" author's words. The answers given would then shape the course of further instruction and discussion.[75]

Preaching

Eventually even preaching itself—the taking of a text, exegeting it, and then applying it—was undertaken by a few Methodist women, a development that only slowly gained acceptance by John Wesley after he personally witnessed the fruits of such activities and saw that it was drawing many people to Christ. In large part because of the example and influence of his mother, Wesley seldom faltered in his conviction that no one, including a woman, should be kept from exercising her liberty of conscience and obeying her inner calling to do the work of God. This belief would later lead him not only to allow but "to encourage the controversial practice of women's preaching."[76] Though he did not officially designate the public speaking of women as preaching for a long time, and in fact avoided it as long as possible, it is interesting that in his journal entry written on August 13, 1746, Wesley does in fact describe one of the women who gave her testimony as a preacher. She met him and the other clergymen who were traveling with him at the door of the church and then followed them to their horses, weeping and praising God. He reports that she "could not refrain from declaring before them all what God had done for her soul. And the words which came from the heart went to the heart. I scarce ever heard such a *preacher* before. All were in tears round about her, high and low; for there was no resisting the Spirit by which she spoke."[77]

Wesley's overwhelmingly positive assessment of her public speech is also an indication of the charismatic nature of such utterances. Had he not firmly believed that the power of the Holy Spirit enabled women as well as men to bear witness to Christ's transforming power in their lives, Wesley would not have given his approval to such unusual activity.[78] In time, this tentative affirmation would lead to his public approbation of the preaching ministries of many women like Sarah Mallet, who described her method by saying:

My way of preaching from the first is to take a text and divide it, and speak from the different heads. For many years when we had but few Chapels in this Country, I preached in the open air and in barns—and in waggons. After I was married, I was with my husband in the preachers plan, for many years. He was a Local Preacher thirty-two years, and finished his work and his life well.[79]

Late in Wesley's life and even after his death, Sarah Mallet preached with this same conviction of God's power at work in her, declaring that neither hell nor death were able to stop her mouth. She affirmed Wesley's support for her activities in a letter to an unknown recipient, calling Wesley a "father" and "faithful friend." Like the other women called to leadership within the Methodist revival, she closely followed his advice for her ministry, finding some people very receptive, but she reported that not all preachers agreed with Wesley. However, Wesley's opinions always carried plenty of weight, and the matter seemed settled when Wesley sent a note via Joseph Harper to Conference in 1787, stating: "We give the right hand of fellowship to Sarah Mallet, and have no objection to her being a preacher in our connection, so long as she preaches the Methodist doctrine, and attends to our discipline."[80]

Sarah went on to express her joy that some Methodist preachers saw fit to encourage female preaching, and she shared her hope that the local and itinerant preachers would meditate on 1 Thessalonians 5:19-20 on not quenching the Spirit and not despising prophesying even if it came from the mouth of a child. If they would only do so, she avows that they would then "be more like Mr. Wesley, and I think more like Christ."[81] And so it was that after decades of women speaking publicly in the aforementioned ways, Sarah Mallet, later Sarah Boyce, was formally authorized to preach by John Wesley and the Manchester Conference of 1787. Upon her husband's death, Sarah and another woman preacher, Martha Grigson, traveled and preached together, demonstrating the importance of the bonds of friendship and mutual support for women engaged in this extraordinary ministry.[82]

Education and Training

Even as far back as the days of the Holy Club in Oxford, Wesley had a great interest in helping ordinary people acquire some level of learning, and he published tracts, pamphlets, sermons, and books at affordable prices so that anyone could have access. In a letter to one George Holder, written November 8, 1790, a few months before his death, Wesley still affirmed the central place of reading, asserting, "It cannot be that the people should grow in grace unless they give themselves to reading. A reading people will always be a knowing people. A people who talk much will know little."[83] One of his most ambitious projects was the compilation of a fifty-volume set of books called *A Christian Library*, and it contained his abridgements of works of practical divinity that he felt would be most helpful.

In particular Wesley desired that his lay preachers be educated and trained for their ministry of public proclamation, and he frequently made practical as well as theological suggestions for ways to improve their preaching. His "1747 Rules for Preaching" included admonishments to begin and end on time and to sing only the hymns that had been approved by Wesley, along with reminders to carry oneself with solemnity during worship, and to be careful not to mispronounce words or use awkward gestures while preaching. He urged them to keep the intended audience in mind and recommended that the plainest text should always be used. He further expected his preachers to be organized enough not to ramble, nor to allegorize or spiritualize the message too much.[84]

His advice was not always welcome nor always followed, but he was determined to give guidelines to increase the lay preachers' effectiveness and to prevent poor preaching from damaging the revival. In a letter of July 28, 1775, to an American itinerant named John King, he wrote:

Always take advice or reproof as a favor; it is the surest mark of love. I advised you once, and you took it as an affront; nevertheless I will do it once more.

Scream no more, at the peril of your soul. God now warns you by me, whom He has set over you. Speak as earnestly as you can, but do not scream. Speak with all your heart, but with a moderate voice. It was said of our Lord, "He shall not cry"; the word properly means, He shall not scream. Herein be a follower of me, as I am of Christ. I often speak loud, often vehemently; but I never scream, I never strain myself. I dare not; I know it would be a sin against God and my own soul. Perhaps one reason why that good man Thomas Walsh, yea and John Manners too, were in such grievous darkness before they died was because they shortened their own lives.

O John, pray for an advisable and teachable temper. By nature you are very far from it; you are stubborn and headstrong. Your last letter was written in a very wrong spirit.[85]

Likewise, he critiqued the preaching and public-speaking skills of the women preachers and exhorters in order to increase their effectiveness. There are striking similarities between the technical advice Wesley gave to John King and his letter of counsel to Sarah Mallet regarding her homiletical style in December 1789.

It gives me pleasure to hear that prejudice dies away and our preachers behave in a friendly manner. . . . Never continue the service above an hour at once, singing, preaching, prayer, and all. You are not to judge by your own feelings, but by the word of God. Never scream. Never speak above the natural pitch of your voice; it is disgustful to the hearers. It gives them pain, not pleasure. And it is destroying yourself. It is offering God murder for sacrifice.[86]

Just like some of their brother preachers, some of the women preachers were uneducated, but many of them were well read in scripture and practical divinity and other subjects. Even though they lacked the opportunity for a formal rhetorical education, their model of preaching was the Oxford-educated John Wesley himself. Wesley placed a high value on education of women as well as men—as

Susanna's son, that is hardly surprising. As a result, he advocated an ambitious course of study for women that was strikingly similar to the one created for the male itinerants, though unlike them, women weren't advised to study foreign languages.[87]

Wesley outlined this "female course of study" in a letter to "Miss L.____ (almost certainly Margaret Lewen), publishing it in the *Arminian Magazine* in 1780, and he sent an almost identical letter to his niece Sarah Wesley in September 1781. First and foremost, Wesley enjoins his readers to pursue the knowledge of God by applying themselves to the Bible, reading and meditating every morning and evening with the aid of his or other commentaries. This intense course was intended only for "those who have a good understanding and much leisure," and it included a wide range of subjects: grammar, arithmetic, geography, logic, natural philosophy, history, metaphysics, poetry, and divinity. Noting it might take three, four, or even five years to read all the suggested books, including Wesley's *Christian Library,* he declared that completion of the course would insure the acquisition of "knowledge enough for any reasonable Christian."[88] It would certainly provide thorough training for anyone daring to preach, male or female.

Disapproval and Repression Following Wesley's Death

John Wesley was led to his appreciation and encouragement of female preaching over a period of years after seeing for himself the good results that came from the testimonies and sermons of women preachers. His goal for the Methodist revival included personal religious experience and its power to transform society as well as individuals; and to further that goal, he was willing to use any practical methods, even if they were unconventional. Paradoxically, his patriarchal and authoritarian rule of the Methodist movement provided space for women to plant seeds in the fertile ground, and his emphasis on the Spirit's role had the effect of undercutting narrow societal expectations of women.[89]

Seeing exceptional women not unlike his mother who were uniquely gifted and called and whose lives and ministries produced fruit, Wesley not only accepted but also promoted their leadership; but not everyone was convinced. A letter written by Joseph Benson while Wesley was still alive is indicative of the negative emotions of some of the male preachers with regard to the rightful place of women in religious leadership positions, and upon Wesley's death, such sentiments only increased.

> It is a shame, 'tis indecent, unbecoming the modesty of the sex for a woman to speak in the church. The actions of the women preachers place their very souls in peril . . . behold the sexes have changed places, the woman is become the head of the man, the men almost all, learn in subjection and the women teach with authority. These things ought not so to be.[90]

After Wesley's death in 1791, disapproval of women's preaching gained even more traction as the more conservative leadership attempted to stifle these Mothers in Israel.[91] As less emphasis was given to the freedom of the Spirit to empower, more stress was placed on conformity, ministerial discipline, and control of the infant Methodist Church.[92] In 1803, the Methodist Conference discussed the thorny question of whether women should be allowed to preach and passed a restrictive resolution citing opposition by some of the people and the surfeit of male preachers.

The resolution did grudgingly allow for a woman receiving an extraordinary call to address other women, but there were nevertheless women who continued to preach in obedience to their call, and a few of them did find ongoing support from those who heard them preach and from some of the itinerants.[93] Mary Bosanquet Fletcher's ongoing preaching ministry and grooming of young female preachers in Madeley was little affected, probably because of her close links to both John Wesley and to her late husband, John Fletcher. Sarah Mallet Boyce continued to preach as well, and her preaching career continued for at least thirty-seven years after this ban.[94]

Despite official disapprobation, male preachers like Zechariah Taft and William Bramwell were supportive of women preachers and strongly encouraged them to use their gifts. In one sermon, Bramwell even asked, "Why are there not more women preachers? Because they are not faithful to their call."[95] Not surprisingly, the women who heard this rebuke recognized in it a call to respond faithfully and not to hide their talents, no matter the consequences. Some of them persevered and continued to speak publicly, even if unofficially, after the ban.

One such gifted woman was Mary Barritt, who was already a well-established evangelist when she later married Zechariah Taft. Encouraged from the early days of her ministry by those who recognized the fruit of her ministry, in the early days of her ministry she received invitations from several well-respected ministers, including John Pawson, Samuel Bradburn, and Alexander Mather. William Bramwell was so supportive of her preaching that he worried her marriage to Taft in 1802 would potentially prevent her from answering her clear call.[96] However, upon their marriage, she accompanied her husband on his preaching circuits and continued to preach despite vociferous disapproval. In her 1827 account of her itinerant preaching ministry, she grieved: "All that I have suffered from the world in the way of reproach and slander, is little in comparison with what I have suffered from some professors of religion, as well as even ministers of the gospel."[97]

The deep-seated antipathy toward a wider and more public ministry for women obviously led to a diminished role for them within Wesleyan Methodism, and their rhetorical activities were glossed over or ignored in official Methodist publications. Pursuant to the policy of editing and managing the role of women in Methodism's story, Leslie Church noted: "In the early years of the nineteenth century obituary notices of certain Methodist women appeared in the *Methodist Magazine* often without any reference to their preaching . . . [an] unfortunate but deliberate policy of omission . . . [which] may have been because the writer, or Jabez Bunting, the Editor, disapproved."[98]

Given this clear direction of Methodism's attempt to distance itself from women's preaching, Sarah Mallet Boyce certainly must have anticipated that her obituary would likewise delete any mention of her preaching from official records. However, she could hardly have anticipated the omission of any obituary of her altogether, but in fact no obituary of Sarah Mallet Boyce was ever printed in any Methodist publication.[99]

Even the more acceptable female activities of spiritual auto-biography and letter writing came under male control as many of their texts were either never published or were heavily edited and compressed into a more "suitable" form.[100] While the official memoirs and autobiographies of women preachers were numerous if perhaps somewhat formulaic, their reliability depended largely on the male editor's or author's opinion about the suitability of women preaching. As a result, if that person opposed the practice, this vital aspect of her life and ministry vanished from the official narrative. As noted, while editor of the *Methodist Magazine*, Jabez Bunting simply omitted any mention of a woman's preaching from her obituary.

In 1825, perceiving a need to preserve the stories of the many women whose ministries were being consigned to oblivion, Mary Barritt Taft's husband Zechariah began preparing a two-volume collection of spiritual autobiographies and biographies, calling it *Biographical Sketches of the Lives and Public Ministry of Various Holy Women, Whose Eminent Usefulness and Successful Labours in the Church of Christ, Have Entitled Them to Be Enrolled Among the Great Benefactors of Mankind.*[101] Taft's work is of lasting importance, as the voices of many of these Methodist women have been muted or drowned out by the men who have largely controlled the narrative. He received and published letters from various women following the publication of the first volume, expressing their grief at being written out of the narrative.[102]

Women's life writing (spiritual autobiographies, letters, tracts, sermons, etc.) provides insight into women's communal identities and friendships within a network of women writing in youth and in old age.[103] The vital role of women's friendships in collecting and preserving spiritual memoirs and other writings can be seen in the case of both Sarah Crosby and Mary Bosanquet Fletcher. Upon her death, Sarah left her manuscript books to her friends Ann Tripp and Elizabeth Mortimer, in expectation of them being published.[104] It took Tripp and Mortimer two years of lobbying before extracts of Crosby's writings were finally published in the *Methodist Magazine*. Her original manuscripts were lost, perhaps deliberately by Joseph Benson during his editing, and because of this, the best record of this prominent female preacher of the early Methodist revival is preserved in her correspondence. Fortunately, Zechariah Taft in his *Biographical Sketches* included excerpts from her journal in which she recorded riding great distances, holding hundreds of meetings, and writing over 116 letters of spiritual advice. He remarked with regret that despite leaving an abundance of writings, when Sarah Crosby died, there was only a brief article in the *Methodist Magazine*.[105]

Having witnessed the mishandling of her friend's memoirs, and with the experience of Benson's liberties with her late husband's manuscripts, Mary Bosanquet Fletcher took precautions to safeguard hers, leaving them to a trusted member of her circle, Mary Tooth. (To Mary Fletcher's dismay, Benson had held the sole copy of John Fletcher's work for over ten years, leaving her helpless to recover it.)

The next chapter will examine the early life and ministry of Mary Bosanquet Fletcher as located within her influential friendship network of women preachers and leaders. Their intimate friendships illustrate the core values of the entire Methodist movement, that of love of God and neighbor, of sanctification and Christian perfection, of social holiness and not merely individual holiness. Phyllis Mack persuasively argues, "There is no example in early Methodism of the attainment of sanctification by a solitary mystic or an individual whose connection to Methodism was institutional but not social. If we want to understand how Methodists loved God, we must first understand how they loved each other."[106]

THREE

Mary Bosanquet and Her Circle of Friends

Faithfully Keeping a Record

"I was born September the first, O.S. 1739, at Laytonstone [sic], in Essex. From my earliest years, I can remember the Spirit of God striving with me, and offering me salvation; but I slighted these most gracious calls, and many times resisted the most tender invitations."[1] Thus begins the spiritual memoirs of an amazing Methodist woman who was a prolific writer of letters, journals, tracts, and sermons, a leader in classes and bands. Like Susanna Wesley before her, Mary Bosanquet eventually found herself filling several important ministry roles. She was an educator and mother to the children in her orphanage and an exhorter and preacher before, during, and after her marriage to Wesley's close friend and her ministry partner, John Fletcher, the Anglican priest of the Madeley parish in Shropshire.[2]

After his death in 1785, she continued to play a key role in the ongoing ministry in Madeley, leading prayer services, catechizing and teaching children and adults, expounding on scripture, and preaching. She ran the Methodist Society there until her own death in 1815, preaching every Sunday in the former tithe barn before leading her congregation to the parish church for worship and sacrament, and she had considerable input and even control over the appointment of curates to the parish church as well as over preachers appointed to her chapel.[3]

Her influence extended far beyond her own place and time, largely because of her deep friendships with Sarah Ryan, Sarah Crosby, Sarah Lawrence, and other Methodist women like Mary Tooth, her spiritual protégé and "daughter."[4] For these reasons, this chapter focuses on Mary Bosanquet Fletcher as the central figure within a sizeable network of early Methodist women leaders and preachers who provided support, friendship, and accountability to each other.[5]

This circle of women around Mary Bosanquet Fletcher was an alternative to the patriarchal model of family; it was a religious community that had female friendship at the heart of its spiritual and literary practice. In writing on the life of her dear friend Sarah Ryan as told to her by Sarah herself, Mary models a pattern found in other manuscripts of early Methodist women who also used a relational mode of writing for the preservation of their collective history.[6]

After Mary Fletcher's death and after the painful experience of seeing Sarah Crosby's work lost, manipulated, and ignored, as well as the treatment of John Fletcher's writings, Mary Tooth was determined to protect Mary Fletcher's legacy, making sure that Henry Moore returned the manuscripts in one piece and with any editorial changes clearly marked. However, when Moore received Mary Fletcher's untitled spiritual autobiography, her *Private Thoughts in the Way of Journal Cross Hall*, and what became known as her *Thoughts on Communion With Happy Spirits*, he made numerous changes by imposing his own pagination, polishing the grammar, deleting repetitive material, and "stitching these manuscripts together."[7]

Moore's deletion of certain sections of Mary's writings offers a "cleaned-up" version of this very real woman whose faith had a strong mystical bent as illustrated in her reflections on her own and others' dreams. Thinking she had few gifts and little grace for public speaking, she often experienced anxiety and doubts when she had to preach in public, despite her firm sense of being called to do so. She recorded in her journal that she had found encouragement in a vivid dream—a detailed and very feminine, maternal dream that Moore completely edited out in the published journal.

In the dream, a man brought a small child to Mary and told her to nurse it. She told the man this was impossible but that she would try anyway. Crying out in pain because she had no milk, she begged him to take the child and feed it until her milk came in, but he insisted that she keep trying, to "let it draw." Obediently, she again began to nurse the child, and to her amazement, she now produced such a flow of milk that she cried out, "Bring me all the children in the world for I have milk enough for them all." Upon awaking, she discerned that those words "let it draw" meant for her to assist and receive everyone who came to her and for her to continue to answer God's call, without waiting for more grace and gifts to appear but using the little she had and trusting that God would increase it. In his article "Mary Fletcher as a Source for Spirituality in Methodism," David Frudd points out that this extract is significant because it draws a comparison between Mary and Wesley, showing her to be a leader in her own right, and he wryly comments that if the world was Wesley's parish, then Mary Bosanquet had milk enough to feed its children.[8]

Moore's evident discomfort with this vivid image of a nursing mother along with his interest in portraying Mary as a model of female modesty and Methodist piety lead him to sanitize her story by removing these down-to-earth references to her sexuality. In doing so, he not only rendered her less human, he critically downplayed her sense of vocation *as a woman* who found great comfort and encouragement from her dream of a very feminine experience. Though Mary Tooth's reaction to Moore's editing of the writings of her "mother" in the faith is not known, it is worth noting that Tooth was reticent about loaning Mary Fletcher's papers to anyone else after Moore returned them.[9]

Determined that the vital roles of Methodist women be known and their stories treasured, Mary Tooth recorded a communal history of Methodism's women preachers, writing consciously to preserve a uniquely female voice from being expunged within a context of marginalization and institutional hostility. The importance of collaborative female relationships in the creation and transmission of a literary tradition across generations in their roles as authors, editors, and spiritual mentors cannot be overstated. Tooth's identity as an author is clearly shaped by an understanding of Methodism as an alternative family extending beyond individual lives. The Methodist revival inculcated an understanding of family that was spiritual rather than biological, and there was frequently a push-pull between familial and religious identities and conflict due to the postponement or rejection of the roles of wife and mother.[10]

Contacts with Methodists, Conflict with Family and Friends

As a young woman and even as a child, Mary Bosanquet experienced tension between her desire to be a dutiful and obedient daughter and her heartfelt commitment to Methodism with its influences that lay outside the family. Born into a family of means, she was a serious child with a deep interest in religious matters; and at the tender age of five, she became concerned about her eternal welfare, asking her father many searching questions as he taught her the catechism. There were times when she felt she relied on Christ with true faith, but more times when she was uncertain of this. A maid in their household who had been converted under the preaching of the Methodists shared her testimony with Mary and her sister, loaning them books.

After her family dismissed the servant and took away her books, Mary felt like a blind person groping her way through the darkness, and in their worry for her well-being, her parents were unsure what to do with her. During this time of turmoil, her sister met and introduced Mary to Mrs. Lefevre, an early and influential member of the Foundry Society in London. She introduced the sisters to a wider circle of Methodist acquaintances, though their parents were unaware of this.[11]

Longing to be assured that her sins had been forgiven, Mary struggled with the question of *how* to know. She devised tests to determine whether or not she had faith or whether Jesus was the Son of God or not, cutting herself severely to see if he would stop the bleeding. Naturally this was disturbing to her family, even though they thought she had done it accidentally.[12] Moore expunged this incident when he edited her writings, though Mary clearly considered it an important event in her spiritual journey, discerningly commenting that children's feelings and spiritual reflections are much deeper than most adults recognize.[13]

Not surprisingly, this agony of spirit and body led to what she called lowness of spirits and weakness of nerves, accompanied by strong temptations and the nagging fear that she had somehow blasphemed against the Holy Spirit. She finally began to receive some relief from her anxiety when her sister responded, "Why, you do not mean to blaspheme, do you?"[14] At her father's prodding, Mary prepared for confirmation, though she felt herself unworthy. She read the confirmation and baptismal vows repeatedly, praying for God to empower her to fulfill them, and this made a deep impression on her.

She was clearly of a mystical disposition, understanding many of her dreams and visions to be messages from God; and, for her, the sacrament of Holy Communion could also be an occasion of feeling the closeness of God's Spirit. After being confirmed she mused, "For some months after, every time I approached the Lord's table, I had a very peculiar sense of his presence, and sometimes I felt as if the Lord Jesus did from his own hand give me the sacred emblems of his body and blood."[15]

She later felt her faith wavering again and recorded herself as becoming insolent and disobedient toward her family, though she found comfort in her friendship with Mrs. Lefevre, who provided her with spiritual guidance and instruction. The conflict between belonging to her family of origin and maintaining spiritual integrity was manifest in her efforts to re-create herself in opposition to her parents and their worldly outlook and environment.[16] When Mary's sister married and left home, Mary felt that she must openly confess and practice her Methodist beliefs, especially when she became convinced of the sinfulness of going with her parents to the theatre.

Torn between what she saw as an absolute duty to her parents and yet understanding that she must obey them "in the Lord," she had a frank but calm conversation with her father, in which he declared that she seemed to think that "all places of diversion" and indeed the "whole spirit of the world" was sinful. Seizing the opportunity to state her determination not to conform to worldly manners or fashions, she assured him that she "would not be disobedient in any thing, unless where conscience made it appear to be my duty."[17] Just as Susanna Wesley had pointed to God as arbiter in her arguments with Samuel, Mary got around her father by appealing to the higher authority they both recognized.[18] These were trying days for her as she met with great opposition for her Methodist leanings and was frequently kept from visiting Mrs. Lefevre, whom she had come to love deeply. However, Mary's mother did allow her to see Mrs. Lefevre on her deathbed, and afterward Mary poured out her heart to the Lord, perceiving Christ as her "robe before the throne of God."[19]

While she and her family were staying in London, she met a young man with marriage on his mind; but more significant, she encountered Sarah Crosby and more Methodists at the home of Dorothy Furley (later Downes). Filled with anticipation, Mary went to hear Sarah speak, and as a result the "affair of the gentleman was obliterated from my mind; and the prospect of a life wholly devoted to God, drank up every other consideration."[20] She and Sarah Crosby began to exchange letters, and Mary felt called to a life of prayer and holiness as an unmarried woman. But even beyond that, she believed God was calling her not simply to holiness but also to some particular ministry, and as she cried out for discernment, she exclaimed:

> I would be given up, both soul and body, to serve the members of Christ. My firm resolution was to be wholly given up to the church, in any way that He pleased. I desired not to be idle, but employed as those described by St. Paul to Timothy, "If she have brought up children, if she have lodged strangers, if she have washed the saints' feet, and diligently followed after every good work." I can hardly express with what power these words would come to my mind. It seemed to me, the Lord had planned out all my way; and I only wished so to walk.[21]

As a result, she declined her parents' invitation to visit Scarborough and remained at her uncle's home in London where she became more involved with members of the Foundry Society. This led her to embrace even stricter principles, including wearing plain, unadorned dresses. One significant new acquaintance was Sarah Ryan, at whose home Sarah Crosby boarded, along with a woman named Mary Clark. Their class met there, and the house became "a little Bethel" to Mary, who stayed there as often as possible.[22]

Upon being reunited with her parents, she fell ill, at least partly because of the terrible strain of being pulled in two different directions between love of her family and her newly awakened faith with a growing sense of being called to fulfill some particular vocation. Away from like-minded spiritual companions to watch over her in love and fearing to disobey her parents, yet fearing even more to disobey God, she endured a time of trial and deep depression. As seventeen-year-old Mary wept before the Lord, she was at last relieved when she encountered "an unusual brightness, (yet not dazzling)," and a voice so powerful that it resonated throughout her body and soul, saying, "Thou shalt walk with me in white." When she replied that she was unworthy, the voice spoke to her again, "Thou shalt walk with me in white; I will make thee worthy. . . . I will thoroughly purge away thy dross, and take away all thy sin."[23] This impressive "manifestation" gave her hope and helped to sustain her during her darkest moments all throughout her life because she never doubted that the voice she heard had indeed come from the Lord. Though she endured other times of oppressive sadness and despair in her personal life and in her ministry, this empowering theophany provided her with "both a vocational trajectory and a theological affirmation of that calling throughout her ministry."[24]

Staying in Bristol to regain her health while her parents spent a season in Bath, she was affirmed and enlightened as she spent time with Methodist friends Dorothy Furley, Sarah Crosby, and Sarah Ryan. However, returning home with her mother and father again incited the tug of war between acceding to her parents' expectations regarding dress and amusements and her growing feeling that holy obedience to God required her to be "clean and neat" while wearing the "plainest things," but she found strength in recalling the words from 1 Peter 3:5: "For so the holy women of old adorned themselves."[25]

The fraught mother-daughter relationship had led Mary's mother more than once to maintain that it would be better for the family if Mary moved out lest she infect her younger brothers by her example and conversation. When her father tried to extract a promise from her that she would not attempt to convert them to her Methodist brand of Christian faith, she respectfully but frankly told him that she could not consent. Reluctantly and without bitterness, her father responded that she was forcing him to make her leave home, though it was another two months before she was compelled to leave. When she did so, she moved into lodgings with her maid in Hoxton Square where her only furniture was two beds and a borrowed table with candlesticks, and her only food was rancid bread and butter.[26] She was invited back home to dine with her family from time to time, and they occasionally provided her with some of the necessities of life, but at age twenty-two, she was supporting herself on an inherited income, free at last to continue building close relationships with other Methodists. This physical removal from family in 1760 was an important step, allowing her to pursue close friendships with like-minded women.

As Mary spent more time with Sarah Ryan, she experienced more of the presence of God, leading her to call her "the friend of my soul."[27] As did many Methodists, she began to envision family in terms of her friendships with other Methodists rather than defined by her former ties to mother, father, and siblings, even replacing her family of origin with new mothers, sisters, and brothers. Mary's disappointing and tense relationship with her own mother laid the foundation for a deep attachment to Sarah Ryan that led her to declare that the Lord had given Sarah to Mary as a mother.[28] In her journal Mary wrote that she wanted Sarah's maternal advice for figuring out what her own rules and activities should be, and it was as a mother that Sarah wrote to her band in London, addressing them as her "dear children," adding that she was in "travail in birth till Christ be formed in your hearts."[29]

The Methodist revival was gathering momentum in London and elsewhere, and Mary was inspired not only by her relationships with women like Sarah Ryan and the preaching of John Wesley and Thomas Maxfield but also by the example of "simple persons, both men and women" who were declaring that the kingdom of heaven was at hand.[30] At a class meeting with her Methodist "family" that lasted four hours, she wrestled with a sense of discouragement, praying that she might love God with all her heart. A Brother Gilford was also praying for her, and she felt a calmness that spread through her spirit, and she "laid hold on Jesus as [her] full Saviour," repeating in her heart, "Thy will be done." She also took heart from Isaiah's words "In returning and rest shall ye be saved; in quietness and confidence shall be thy strength."[31] Many passages of scripture were a source of grace and strength for her, as were the many hymns of Charles Wesley, and she frequently drew comfort and felt invigorated by repeating his words "Having done all, by faith I stand,/ And give the praise, O Lord, to thee;/ Thy holy arm, thy own right hand/ Hath got thyself the victory."[32]

Interestingly, her record of her experience of assurance sounds similar to John Wesley's; both of them felt a sense of unspeakable peace afterward. Mary soon began to experience intense feelings upon observing suffering among other people and the oppression of animals, especially horses and dogs. Like Sarah Ryan, using a strikingly feminine image to describe this, she said, "I seemed to groan and travail in birth, as it were, for the whole creation."[33] Finding that she was no longer filled with fear, she used another feminine metaphor, declaring that "the Lord kept me, as to outward things, like an infant in its mother's arms."[34] However, in taking her spiritual exercises a little too far, particularly fasting, she experienced some physical complaints that were eased by the gift of port wine from her earthly father. Again and again in her journal, she praised God for supplying her need.

Stepping Out in Faith, Establishing a New Family

Sarah Ryan had been appointed as housekeeper at the New Room in Bristol but had recently left this position due to poor health, and she and Mary exchanged affectionate letters before Sarah moved to London to live with her sister. Both were ill, and despite her much higher social status, Mary nursed both Sarah and her sister back to health because she was concerned that they only had one servant to care for them. Knowing her need for a spiritual companion in her Christian journey and valuing Sarah Ryan's religious experience and counsel, she proposed that they begin sharing a home.

Sharing, in her words, one heart, mind, and habitation, Mary was so drawn to Sarah that she felt death itself could not possibly dissolve their unity of spirit. In 1762, with a legacy from Mary's grandmother, they started a quasi-monastic community that was both boarding school and home for destitute orphans on some property in Leytonstone near Mary's parents.[35] This orphanage and school, modeled on the Kingswood School near Bristol, received Wesley's warm approval. On December 1, 1764, he expressed his delight: "M[ary] B[osanquet] gave me a further account of their affairs at Leytonstone. . . . What will be does not yet appear."[36] Mary worried about the effect her association with the Methodists might have on her parents since they lived so near, but just as before, she felt the words of Jesus saying, "He that loveth father or mother more than me, is not worthy of me."

When her father told her he had no objection to her establishing her boarding school so close to her childhood home, he warned that others might not be so tolerant and that he would be powerless to stop a mob from pulling the house down around her. She received another dream in which Jesus appeared to her simply as a man dressed in white rather than in a dazzling display of light and majesty, and she could sense his purity and holiness as he came close to her. She heard him clearly say to her, "I will send thee to a people that are not a people, and I will go with thee. Bring them unto me, for I will lay my hand upon them and heal them. Fear not, only believe."[37]

On March 24, 1763, Mary Bosanquet and Sarah Ryan moved to Leytonstone and quickly determined to spend an hour every night together in prayer and in spiritual reading. Initially Mary, Sarah, and the maid were the only occupants until Sarah Ryan's orphaned niece Sarah Lawrence, usually called Sally, came to live there and became as a daughter to Mary Bosanquet. In time, between 1763 and 1768, at least thirty-four adults and thirty-five children were part of this household, including Sarah Crosby and Ann Tripp, who were both class leaders and early female preachers.[38] Ann Tripp acted as governess to the children, while Sarah Crosby was often away preaching and meeting with classes, and their household became a little community composed of a school, an orphanage, a hospital, and a home for poor widows.[39]

Sarah Ryan's complicated marital history had made her a controversial figure, while her ministry as a class leader and public speaker along with her claim to spiritual perfection made her a well-known and honored figure within Methodism. She was also a close friend and frequent correspondent of John Wesley even though his wife, Molly, publicly addressed her as a "whore" and accused her of being Wesley's mistress.[40] As Sarah later related it to Mary Bosanquet, Sarah had previously confided in Molly Wesley about her marital misadventures, only to be humiliated at a dinner for sixty or seventy preachers when Mrs. Wesley loudly announced, "See that whore, who is serving you. She hath three husbands now alive."[41] As Molly continued her tirade, Sarah apparently sank into a chair and closed her eyes, quietly accepting it as divine justice for her past sin and enduring it like a lamb led mute to the slaughter. It is not clear how the others reacted.[42]

Despite this kind of harsh or negative reaction, the early Methodist women leaders and preachers regarded answering their perceived call from God as much more important than ostracism or humiliation. They were neither interested in remaining confined within strict social conventions nor in turning the social order on its head. Quite simply, their desire to follow God's command was their trump card when challenged and their comfort when anxious.[43]

In her narrative, Mary describes the administration of the boarding school and establishment of a Methodist society there as a collaborative venture between herself and Sarah Ryan with herself the junior partner. Sensitive to criticism of her friend and spiritual mother Sarah, and partly because the money for their venture all came from Mary's inheritance, Mary insisted that despite her ill health, Sarah Ryan was the mainspring of their work and that it would have been impossible for her to have acted without Sarah as she herself had neither grace nor ability for it.[44] Mary admitted that the ideas and plans generally came from her but insisted they would not have prospered without Sarah's diligence, firm resolve, and practical life experience as someone who had always worked to support herself.

Shortly after their arrival at the Leytonstone property, the Cedars, a poor woman of Mary's acquaintance asked if she could join them at their prayer meetings, and then she showed up with two or three friends at their Thursday evening gathering. To Mary's surprise, before she knew it, there were twenty-five in attendance, and as more began to come, Sarah and Mary decided to speak individually to each one. A few were offended by this and stopped coming, but among others, there was a hunger for more spiritual depth, so they agreed to meet on Tuesday nights while keeping Thursday evenings for the more public gathering. Because they had a core group and were still growing, they applied to John Wesley for a preacher, so he sent a Mr. Murlin to them the following Sunday, and such signs of growth naturally led to more opposition and even to threats of violence.

On one occasion, during the Thursday evening gathering, four men carrying large sticks showed up at the back door, frightening her servant. Mary's response was that she and her companions were not worried about mobs while going about the Master's business, and she continued with the meeting until she had concluded addressing the subject. Only then did she speak to the men, offering them a copy of the rules of the society. Mary's laconic record of this episode concludes, "We heard no more of the mob. At this time the hand of the Lord was much with us, supporting and comforting us under every trial." Unfortunately, at other times, mobs would gather in the dark on Sunday evenings, throwing dirt at the members of the society, coming into the yard and breaking things, and howling and roaring at the unshuttered windows.[45]

Determined to educate and house destitute orphans as well as care for the adults of the household, they established rules for the duties and employments of the children and themselves, creating for everyone a sort of uniform dress made from dark purple cotton. The children were taught good manners and religion, and because they would have to support themselves in the future, they were taught reading, writing, and arithmetic, as well as domestic skills such as cooking, sewing, and nursing. The children's time was very structured. They rose early for prayer, breakfast, and work, met for instruction from 8 a.m. until noon, ate at 1 p.m., resumed class from 2 p.m. until 5 p.m., and there was a little free time allotted for recreation or walking. They ate supper, had family prayer, and were to be in bed by 8 p.m.[46]

There were some perhaps unconscious echoes of Susanna Wesley's child-rearing methods and a very deliberate imitation of the pattern of Francke's much-admired orphanage at Halle, Germany. The physical health of the children and clothing and feeding them came first, followed by showing "love to their souls and bodies." Also like Francke, their household had a poor box installed so that visitors could make a donation for the maintenance of the children, which Mary reluctantly agreed to allow, partly because she worried about her family's possible objections and partly because she recognized that it was always easier for her to give than to receive.[47]

In her private writings, Mary called herself "the Lord's innkeeper" and the spiritual mother of the little community, as well as a pillar in God's house.[48] Apparently seeing the Cedars in that same light, John Wesley approvingly called their household a little family and commented in his journal (February 12, 1767), "I preached at Leytonstone. Oh, what a house of God is here. Not only for decency and order, but for the life and power of religion. I am afraid there are very few such to be found in all the King's dominions."[49] His journal entry after his return visit in November 1767 was similarly wholehearted and positive: "How good it would be for me to be here, not twice in a year, but in a month."[50]

New Griefs and Relocation

A devout young woman named Miss Lewen came to board at the Cedars, and she decided to make a will, leaving a considerable amount of money to Mary Bosanquet, making Mary quite uneasy. As Miss Lewen's health deteriorated, she again spoke of giving Mary two thousand pounds, an immense amount of money, for the use of the household, despite her protests. Upon Miss Lewen's death, however, Mary burned the will, not wanting to be accused of unduly influencing her friend. Unfortunately, she was not only reproached for Miss Lewen's desire to honor her with the bequest but also accused of killing Miss Lewen by "rigorous mortification," the same charge that was laid at Wesley's door upon the death of his friend Richard Morgan at Oxford.[51] Both of Mary's parents died around that same time, and Sarah Ryan's health grew steadily worse, prompting Mary, in 1768, to seek out a house and farmland in Yorkshire, hoping to improve Sarah's health and find a cheaper place to live. Sadly, aged only forty-four, Sarah Ryan was so weak and ill that she died shortly after the move in August 1768 and was buried with her name and age followed by the words "who lived and died a Christian" on her gravestone.[52]

Sorrowing over the death of this soul friend and spiritual mother with whom she had shared "emotions, spiritual purpose, finances, and home," Mary became ill herself.[53] She had called their relationship a union that not even death could dissolve, but in Sarah's absence she felt overwhelmed at the prospect of now overseeing every aspect of the household of thirty persons on her own. Their intimate friendship had been marked by a mutual confession of sins and the sharing of spiritual experiences that was characteristic of the Methodist practice of telling the story of one's spiritual journey. No wonder she felt lost without this friend of her soul.[54]

Mary had been accustomed to managing the household's spiritual and financial affairs, the education of the children, meeting individually with each member of the family, sharing duties associated with the care of the society meetings, and caring for the sick, all of which was tremendously taxing. Now on top of that, she had the responsibility of all the practical matters of caring for the kitchen, buying stores, managing the needle-work and other domestic affairs that were beyond her experience, and management of the farm. She was sharply criticized for bad cooking and unwise purchases by members of the household and smugly scolded in letters by family and friends because of her move to Yorkshire. But her friends the Taylors initially proved to be helpful to her as she tried to get settled at Cross Hall.[55]

However, there were new trials seemingly around every corner. Her farm manager was unreliable and the farm itself unprofitable, she continued to suffer from ill health and the attentions of an unwelcome suitor, and her spiritual life was filled with dramatic ups and downs.[56] Happily, her friend Sarah Crosby had joined her household, and she had stirred a great desire for revival in Yorkshire after telling people there about the work of sanctification taking place in London, leading the two women to begin holding society meetings that grew rapidly and spread. They were good friends, and yet Mary missed the special intimacy of her relationship with her deceased friend Sarah Ryan. In her journal, Mary describes fellow Christians such as Sarah Crosby as "kind friends," but she felt that no one could provide the friendship she particularly craved.[57] She mourned for her faithful friend, saddened that even though she knew some of the "excellent of the earth" who lived under her own roof, including Sarah Crosby, she felt that "friendship is so immediately the gift of God, we cannot form it when we will. There must be a similitude of mind, a something which God alone can give, and which he at this time was pleased to withhold from me, perhaps that I might learn to depend on himself alone."[58]

As the numbers of society members increased, Mary, being one of the main leaders, was asked to share her observations or rules for meetings with the "fixed leaders" of the smaller offshoots. First, she cautioned them that only those steadily seeking after Christian perfection be admitted. Second, she urged them always to come in the lively expectation that their faith would be increased; third, that they bear with each other's mistakes or infirmities in love as a parent does with a child. Her fourth rule was a warning against evil-speaking and gossip, particularly when aimed at the king or at their spiritual leaders. Fifth, she encouraged them to hold fast to truth and to keep their consciences clear. Her sixth rule amounts to a vigorous defense of Christian perfection using the Church of England's baptismal and confirmation vows as supportive statements, while the seventh word of advice was to keep one's eyes firmly fixed on Christ and rooted in him the living vine. Her eighth observation was encouragement to remember that they were united by a holy covenant to God and to each other, which necessitated the setting of a good example for anyone observing their life or conversation so that onlookers might be encouraged to seek Christian holiness for themselves.[59]

In her concern for leading her household, especially as a spiritual director, Mary's thoughts echo those of Susanna Wesley before her. She carefully considered the family rules, praying for God's guidance in helping to correct and instill in them the things of God. She concludes that in order for her to be the head of the community in a way that is pleasing to God, she "must have no spring of action but love." Whether in good health or high spirits or in sickness or distress, the spirit of love was the needful attribute for her to fulfill her place in their lives as a mother.[60]

She decided to meet with the family at stated regular times in order to be sure that the "sweet harmony of love" was at work in their midst, asking for them to relay specific concerns to her regarding saving money, redeeming the time, and doing all things well. She warned the family just as she had warned society members about the importance of guarding the tongue and taking care not to offend in word, and she proposed that they enter into a time of fasting and special prayer.[61] Despite her continuing grief over Sarah Ryan's death, assisted by Sarah Crosby, Mary also assumed the mantle and role of a "Mother in Israel" as she nurtured other women with her wisdom, companionship, experience, and fortitude.

Sarah Crosby, Wesley's First Female Preacher

Ten years older than Mary Bosanquet, Sarah Crosby was one of the earliest and most prominent of the women preachers of Methodism, a well-respected leader who corresponded frequently and extensively with John Wesley over a period of many years. Wesley treated her, Sarah Ryan, and Mary Bosanquet as colleagues and spiritual comrades, even allowing them some freedom to criticize and question him with regard to his spiritual life.[62] Converted in 1749, she was first introduced to John Wesley's *Appeals to Men of Reason and Religions* and his sermon on a "Catholic Spirit" by the man she later married and who deserted her in 1757.[63]

Sarah heard George Whitefield preach in London in 1750, and because she was greatly persuaded by his Calvinistic understanding of the faith, she was initially somewhat prejudiced against John Wesley though intrigued with his teaching on Christian perfection. Before he left for Ireland in February 1757, she heard him preach at the Foundry, reflecting in her journal that he did so "with no power." She frequently heard and was comforted by the preaching of Charles Wesley, and upon reading John Wesley's sermon on Christian perfection, she began to believe that God could and would make her perfect. Upon his return, she confessed her former opinion of him and, as a result of their talk, joined the society in October, receiving her class ticket from Wesley himself. She began to seek entire sanctification and then became a class leader in 1752.[64]

At Wesley's request, she prepared a deeply personal spiritual narrative dated August 17, 1757. In it, she candidly speaks of her struggles. Desiring to be filled with this perfect love described by John and Charles Wesley, she had instead become increasingly convinced of her sinfulness.[65] The doubts and temptations she had suffered prior to her experience of assurance now reappeared, and these afflictions coupled with her constant labor and the stringent abstinence she practiced left her physically weak and ill.[66] However, in the midst of this time of suffering, she was often comforted and blessed by reading John Wesley's sermons and from reading and singing Charles Wesley's hymns. One day while she was working, she saw Jesus in the "eye of my mind" and was submerged in his love. She was so overcome that she felt

Constrain'd to cry, by love divine,
My God! Thou art for ever mine.[67]

This occurred around the time she became a class leader, a task of which she felt unworthy. As she prayed, she received yet another vision in which she found herself being overwhelmed by the power of God, sensing that Christ was standing before her. As he stood there, she confessed her willingness to follow him even unto death. His response was to direct her to feed his sheep.[68] Her soul was set at rest, and her heart filled with peace and love as she realized that some of what she had thought were sins were instead merely temptations and that God could and would remove the root of sin from her heart. Being assured of the Spirit's power and promise to dwell within her, she no longer feared sharing the good news of the change wrought in her soul, and she felt a fresh reminder of the Spirit when she did so. She records, "I walked in light and liberty and, blessed be God, continue to do so, but I long for more. Frequently he assures me he will manifest himself more fully than he has yet done. This I am waiting for. . . ."[69] She would not have long to wait.

Given the description of her piety and leadership by Frances Mortimer, who later married Methodist preacher John Pawson, it is not surprising that Sarah Crosby would enlarge the range of rhetorical activities of women to eventually include preaching: "I cannot repeat all the good things I heard from Mrs. Crosby, Mrs. Downes, and others. I can only add, that those little parties, and classes and bands, are the beginning of the heavenly society in this lower world."[70] In her diary, Frances Mortimer Pawson recollected the techniques by which Sarah Crosby conducted her meetings with the bands and classes: "She did not always approve of exhorting persons to believe, and believe; but rather [sought] to find out the hindrances of their faith. They should then be exhorted to lay those hindrances all aside and pray the Holy Spirit so to shine on their mind that they may see the little foxes which spoil the vine."[71]

Sarah also possessed a reputation for her gift of praying, which Frances Mortimer Pawson much admired, writing, "She used to begin prayer with the simplicity of a little child, and then rise to the language of a mother of Israel. Thus she prayed with the spirit and with the understanding."[72] After hearing her preach on December 1, 1774, Frances wrote, "Mrs. Crosby expounded the 13th chapter of the first epistle to the Corinthians. She explained the characters of divine charity, or love, with a simplicity I had never heard before. Her heart and words acted in concert. Every sentence was impressive, and carried conviction to the heart, . . . My soul panted for that love on which she so delightfully expatiated."[73]

In 1759, Sarah became acquainted with a young woman named Mrs. Dobinson and invited her to join her class. Largely because of Sarah's prayers, conversation, and guidance, Mrs. Dobinson did join and became an eager convert. Early in 1761, with Sarah Crosby's support and encouragement, Mrs. Dobinson and her husband made the bold decision to move from London to Derby with the express desire to establish a Methodist society there, an action that helped create the chain of events that led directly to Methodist women preaching.[74] Because she experienced an inner witness that was an intense call to speak publicly, even though neither of them called it preaching at this time, Sarah Crosby is often considered the first woman Wesley ever authorized to preach.[75]

On February 8, 1761, there was a momentous shift in the public ministry of women within the Methodist revival. Prepared to meet with a class of twenty-seven people, Sarah Crosby was faced with a dilemma when she saw how many more had come. How could she possibly speak to each person individually as she usually did, and yet how could she turn away from their very real spiritual needs? Realizing it would be impractical even to try to converse one-on-one and being concerned about propriety, she nevertheless felt it her duty to speak to them publicly. In her journal she records her somewhat ambivalent feelings about the experience:

> This day my mind has been calmly stayed on God. In the evening I expected to meet about thirty persons in class;

but to my great surprise there came near two hundred. I found an awful, loving sense of the Lord's presence, and much love to the people: but was much affected both in body and soul. I was not sure if it was right for me to exhort in so public a manner, and yet I saw it impracticable to meet all these people by way of speaking particularly to each individual. I, therefore, gave out a hymn, and prayed, and told them part of what the Lord had done for myself, persuading them to flee from all sin.[76]

Concerned that she might have overstepped her bounds, she immediately wrote to John Wesley, asking for his advice concerning this unexpected turn of events, yet she was not fearful of his response partly because she felt she was answering a call from God and also partly because of the unwavering encouragement and friendship Wesley had always shown her. Interestingly—and tellingly—even before receiving his reply, she publicly exhorted again on February 13. Because she was even more convinced of the presence of the Lord and mindful of the people's hunger for God, in her journal she recorded a deep inner sense of the rightness of her actions:

This day being appointed for a public fast, I humbled myself in prayer. In the evening I exhorted nearly two hundred people to forsake their sins, and shewed them the willingness of Christ to save. They flock as doves to the windows, tho' as yet we have no preacher. Surely, Lord, thou hast much people in this place. My soul was much comforted in speaking to the people, as my Lord has removed all my scruples respecting the propriety of my acting thus publickly.[77]

On February 14, Wesley responded reassuringly to her letter, offering counsel that both maintained a conservative line against women preaching while tacitly acknowledging her call and authorizing her to share her experience in public. Distinguishing between preaching and acceptable female public speech, the ever-pragmatic Wesley applied "a yard-stick of spiritual expediency" to evaluate the matter.[78]

Hitherto, I think you have not gone too far. You could not well do less. I apprehend all you can do more is, when you meet again, to tell them simply, "You lay me under a great difficulty. The Methodists do not allow of women preachers; neither do I take upon me any such character. But I will just nakedly tell you what is in my heart." This will in a great measure obviate the grand objection and prepare for J. Hampson's coming. I do not see that you have broken any law. Go on calmly and steadily. If you have time, you may read to them the *Notes* on any chapter before you speak a few words, or one of the most awakening sermons, as other women have done long ago.[79]

His suggestion that she read to them from his *Notes on the New Testament* or from the most awakening sermons as other women had done was a clear allusion to Susanna Wesley's activities in the Epworth Rectory when he was a small child, and Sarah did not hesitate to act upon his advice and respond to her sense of call. She met with two classes, visited a dying person, and engaged in a good deal of serious conversation with friends on February 18, again perceiving God's presence. On Good Friday, which fell on March 20, she met with a group and read a sermon appropriate to the occasion to them, retiring that night "weary but happy in God." Two days later on Easter morning, she felt unwell but was aware of God's presence during family prayer and felt herself growing stronger later that evening as she exhorted and prayed for sinners to turn to God.[80]

A few months later, Wesley wrote a letter in much the same vein to another female class leader, Grace Walton, who had apparently had a similar experience. It survives only in a defective state and is dated September 8, 1761.

If a few more Persons come in when you are meeting, [you may] enlarge four or five Minutes . . . [or give] a short Exhortation (perhaps for five or six minutes) [and then] sing & pray: This is going as far as I think any Woman [should do.] For the Words of the Apostle are clear. I think . . . [that his] meaning is this: "I suffer not a woman to teach in a [public congregation, nor thereby to usurp Authority over the man."[81]

Wesley carefully justified their public speaking by drawing a distinction between testimony and exhortation, and preaching itself, which he defined as taking a text and speaking from it.[82] Whether or not he fully realized it, he was leaving the door open for arguments for female preaching, because his note on 1 Corinthians 14:34 admits of some exceptions to the prohibition against their public testimony. This was a point upon which Methodist women would build and upon which Mary Bosanquet would carefully craft her argument for women's extraordinary call to preach in a letter of crucial importance in 1771. Wesley's commentary explicitly states that women should be silent in the churches, "unless they are under an extraordinary impulse of the Spirit," because they are ordinarily not permitted to speak or teach in public assemblies but are to be subject to the man whose job it is to lead and instruct the congregation.[83]

Sarah Crosby continued her public witness when she moved with Mary Bosanquet and Sarah Ryan from Leytonstone to Cross Hall in Yorkshire, and Wesley wrote to her on March 18, 1769, to offer additional advice about her public speaking. Her reputation had preceded her as she had spent time in Yorkshire previously, and many who had heard her were much affected and agreed to meet together every two weeks for prayer.[84] Meanwhile, Wesley was still intent on avoiding the word "preaching" for the activities of women like Grace Walton and Sarah Crosby. Much as he had carefully attempted to deflect criticism by distinguishing the public speech of his male itinerants from actual preaching decades before, he gives a precise description of preaching in the letter, telling her how to avoid actually doing it:

I advise you, as I did Grace Walton, formerly, (1) Pray in public or in private as much as you can. (2) Even in public you may properly enough intermix *short exhortations* with prayer; but keep as far from what is called preaching as you can; therefore never take a text; never speak in a continued discourse without some break, about four or five minutes.

Tell the people, "We shall have another *prayer meeting* at such a time and place."[85]

Mary Bosanquet and the "Extraordinary" Call

Mary Bosanquet and Sarah Crosby continued exhorting and meeting with classes and bands and traveled around Yorkshire and beyond, often accompanying a male itinerant. Other Methodist women were engaged in similar activities elsewhere, and John Wesley's views on women's preaching continued to undergo a transformation. He may have hoped that his careful distinctions between acceptable modes of public speech and unacceptable forms would deflect criticism, but the issue refused to die, and Methodist women refused to disobey the call of God.

Inevitably, this was one of the issues that cropped up at the preachers' Conference meeting at Manchester in August 1765. One of the official questions had to do with Paul's words in 1 Corinthians 14:35 mandating that women keep quiet and ask their husband questions at home. It asked: "But how can we encourage the women in the Bands to speak since 'It is a shame for women to speak in the Church'?"[86]

Still wanting to keep a distinction between the various types of public utterance that were acceptable for women, Wesley walked a tightrope with his careful, even evasive reply—no doubt due to the slow transformation of his views on the subject and the exchange of letters between him and women like Sarah Crosby to whom he had given cautious approval after seeing the fruits of their labors.

A. I deny, 1, That speaking here means any other than speaking as a public teacher. This St. Paul suffered not, because it implied "usurping authority over the man," I Tim.ii,12. Whereas no authority either man or woman is usurped, by the speaking now in question. I deny, 2. That the Church in that text, means any other than in the great congregation.[87]

Not surprisingly, Sarah Crosby continued her labors with Wesley's approval, even when he was excluded from preaching at a parish church because the congregation believed he had permitted Sarah Crosby to preach at Huddersfield, despite her insistence that she was not, in fact, preaching. Wesley's mild response was to write to her that "he did not mind that, for he had places enough to preach in."[88] But the issue simply would not go away, and in the summer of 1771, Mary Bosanquet wrote a remarkable letter to John Wesley explaining the resistance she was facing and requesting his advice, probably hoping for his official approval. Because of its enormous impact, it deserves a close examination.

In her letter, Mary portrays herself as a submissive, humble woman willing to be directed by her leader but then cogently articulates a well-thought-out argument in favor of women's preaching.[89] In other words, she has thought this through carefully but wants to see if Wesley concurs with her, trusting that God will make him her "Director in this thing, so as to remove my scruples one way or the other."[90] She refers to the prayer meetings that she, Sarah Ryan, and Sarah Crosby had led and reminds Wesley that as the frequency of these meetings increased, so did the number of attendees, particularly the "hundreds of carnal persons coming to them, who would not go near a preaching-house; and it is enough to say God was with us and made it known by the effects in many places."[91]

Spiritual fruit was being produced, and it was evident to everyone, but not everyone approved. Some of the lay preachers opposed women speaking in church, calling it unscriptural and impermissible on account of their consciences. After a number of civil conversations about it, Mary afterward felt that Satan was persuading her to consent to their interpretation, but after further prayer and study of the Bible, she came to a quite different conclusion on the matter.

> However, on weighing the thing before the Lord, I think it appears to me thus: I believe I am called to do all I can for God, and in order thereto, I may both sing, pray and converse with them, when I am asked to go with Br. T. to a prayer meeting. I may both sing, pray and converse with them, either particularly, or in general, according to the numbers. Likewise . . . I believe I may speak to the people

and pray with them. . . . I believe I may go as far as I have mentioned above.[92]

Some of the preachers insisted that scripture is clear that a woman is forbidden to teach or be in a position of authority over a man. Mary interpreted the text differently, saying that it forbids a woman to assume authority over her husband but that the ban to women speaking only applies to matters of church discipline or other related matters in the church. Then she emphatically adds, "I do not apprehend it means that she shall not entreat sinners to come to Jesus, nor say, Come, and I will tell you what God has done for my soul."[93] She further points out the logical inconsistency of taking these passages literally because to forbid women to speak in any way in church would make these texts contradict Paul's directions in 1 Corinthians 11:5 in which women are commanded not to prophesy with their heads uncovered, which is of course a type of public speech.[94]

Mary's letter was the first serious defense of women's preaching in Methodism, marked by sound critical scrutiny of the Bible and cogent, persuasive reasoning. On the basis of her thorough examination and extensive exegesis of scripture and the evidence of the transformed lives that resulted from women's preaching, Mary Bosanquet considered six main objections, concluding that women were occasionally called to preach in extraordinary situations.[95] Wesley himself had recognized that God was blessing their work with a harvest of souls, perceiving that the Lord was indeed "owning" their ministries.[96] She ended by asserting that while not every woman was called to preach, neither was every man but that "some have an extraordinary call to it, and woe be to them if they obey it not."

How did she come to this conclusion? Using a question-and-answer format, she directly addresses the six main objections. By looking at the Pauline prohibitions in context, she demonstrates that a proper interpretation of the passages does not preclude women's public speaking in church.[97] She anticipates the objection and answers it:

Ob: – She may [speak] now and then, if under a peculiar
impulse, but never else.

An: – But how often is she to feel this impulse? Perhaps
you will say, two or three times in her life; perhaps
God will say, two or three times in a week, or day—and
where shall we find the Rule for this?

The next objection seems partly rooted in jealousy. She is
reproached for lower attendance figures at the meetings led by
men, saying that it will cause the preachers to be embarrassed.
Her response is empathetic but emphatic—she is sorry if only forty
show up for the preaching, but if one hundred people who normally
avoid the church now attend the prayer meetings, she is thrilled.
She diffidently suggests that people come for the novelty of seeing
a woman in such a role rather than because there is any excellence
in her leadership at the meetings.[98] Related to this objection is a
complaint that the people won't have time to come to their gatherings if they come to hers.

In response to the indignant reproach that female preaching is
in contradiction to rules of modesty for women, she meets them
head-on by pointing out that purity and humility are the characteristics of modesty and that when one endeavors to remain unknown,
as she and the women preachers do, there is no conflict. She turns
to scripture again to make her point: "Now I do not apprehend
Mary sinned against either of these heads, or could in the least be
accused of immodesty, when she carried the joyful news of her
Lord's Resurrection and in that sense taught the Teachers of Mankind. Neither was the woman of Samaria to be accused of immodesty when she invited the whole city to come to Christ."[99]

Mary clearly sees herself and the other female preachers as following in the footsteps of these women in the Bible. She continues
with more examples, saying that none were immodest, just as the
wise woman in 2 Samuel 20:16-22 and Deborah the judge were
not immodest when they spoke and acted in public. All of them
were displaying purity and humility before God.

As she lists the next objection, she hangs the answer upon the idea of an extraordinary call; and whether or not she was conscious of it, her words are in some sense an echo of Susanna Wesley's letter to Samuel when she declared her desire not to neglect the "opportunity of doing good to souls" through her prayer meetings.

> Ob: – But all these were extraordinary calls; sure you will not say yours is an extraordinary call?
> An: – If I did not believe so, I would not act in an extraordinary manner. I do not believe every woman is called to speak publicly, no more than every man to be a Methodist preacher, yet some have an extraordinary call to it, and woe be to them if they obey it not.
> Ob: – But do you believe you have this public call?
> An: – Not as absolute as some of the others, nevertheless, I feel a part of it, and what little I see to be my call, I dare not leave undone.[100]

She disarms the opposition by agreeing that it is surely an extraordinary call of God that impels a woman to preach, but she asserts that she—and surely all Christians—should be unwilling to pass unbelievers by without offering them a chance to hear the gospel, whether it be from the lips of a lay preacher, a woman, or a clergyman.[101] Acknowledging that she has taken up a great deal of Wesley's time by writing such a detailed narrative, Mary then states that she will follow his direction in the matter. She expresses her concern for a Mr. Oliver, an itinerant preacher who was having problems on account of his support for her and the other women preachers, remarking that she appreciates and values him for having a loving spirit and for preaching animating, profitable sermons. Her closing remarks bookend the beginning of her letter as she again expresses her desire to know and do God's will: "I praise my God; I feel him very near, and I prove His faithfulness every day, but I want to live as I do not, and to feel every moment that word."[102]

Mary Bosanquet Fletcher's letter is so significant not only because it is the first sustained argument in favor of women's public speech but also because her exposition of scripture challenged the inconsistencies of her opponents' interpretation. Her approach is not simply a rhetorical device; it reveals and demonstrates her understanding of scripture and how it could be used to defend its own promises in Galatians 3:28. She builds on the common understanding that the speech of the converted relies on biblical language and allusion to express what God has done for their souls. By emphasizing the fact that using scripture to share one's faith is not exceptional but rather is commonplace among common Methodist believers, she implies that there is only a thin line between this type of speech and "taking a text" and expounding or preaching upon it.[103]

While Wesley's views had been undergoing a slow modification for several years as he observed the ministries of women around the Connexion and as he witnessed firsthand the usefulness of their work in proclaiming the gospel, it is also true that he found Mary's mode of arguing an extraordinary call persuasive. His letter in response clearly illustrates the way in which he was still "struggling to accommodate the preaching of women which was apparently owned of God, to the pattern of his ecclesiastical system."[104]

In this monumental letter, Wesley attempts to hold those fruits produced by their ministry and Mary Bosanquet's sensible, biblically astute exegesis in tension with a more traditional understanding. Leslie Church wittily remarks: "It was impossible for him to forbid or discountenance her work, but it was hard for him to acknowledge it."[105] Nevertheless, writing from Londonderry on June 13, 1771, Wesley affirms her understanding of her call and that of certain other women:

> I think the strength of the cause rests there, on your having an *Extraordinary Call.* So, I am persuaded, as every one of our Lay preachers; otherwise I could not countenance this preaching at all. It is plain to me that the whole Work of God termed Methodism is an extraordinary dispensation of His Providence. Therefore I do not wonder if several things occur therein which do not fall under ordinary rules of discipline. St. Paul's ordinary rule was, "I permit not a woman

to speak in the congregation." Yet, in extraordinary cases he made a few exceptions; at Corinth, in particular.[106]

In accepting and approving these irregular preaching activities of women like Mary Bosanquet and Sarah Crosby, Wesley had in some sense crossed the Rubicon. However, it was a natural extension of his thought and practice since he had asserted in *A Farther Appeal to Men of Reason and Religion* that the very act of reading a sermon or scripture text publicly was in itself preaching.[107] In the *Appeal*, in response to the objection that laymen are not permitted to preach in public worship in England, Wesley retorts that it is a common practice for a parish clerk to read one of the scripture lessons of the day during worship and in some cases even to read the entire service, and he rhetorically asks, what is preaching but publishing the Word of God?[108]

By basing his approbation on the same logic he applied to justify his own many irregularities of church discipline, particularly the preaching of his male itinerants, he had opened the door to encourage more women to pursue public speaking activities, despite the disapproval of Church or State.[109] He had furthermore done so in this letter by citing an apostolic, biblical precedent.[110] In an accompanying letter on the same page but addressed to Sarah Crosby, Wesley explicitly counsels her to base her discourses on biblical texts and apparently refers again to his being banned from preaching because of his support of women's activities.[111] He advises:

Reading a chapter or part of one and making short observations may be as useful as any way of speaking. I doubt whether at that particular time it was advisable for you to go to Huddersfield. But it is past. All that you can do now (if you have not done it already) is to write lovingly to Mr. A-- and simply inform him of those facts, concerning which he was misinformed before. It is not improbable he may then see things clearer; but if he do not, you will have delivered your own soul. And whatever farther is said of you is your cross. Bear it, and it will bear you.[112]

What Happened After the Famous Letter and Wesley's Response?

Surviving letters indicate that Sarah Crosby and John Wesley had a close and candid but not uncritical friendship. He valued her opinion, writing in 1772 to ask if she still understood Christian perfection in the same light as she did ten or twenty years before, especially with regard to his *Plain Account of Christian Perfection*. In her letter of response, written January 26, 1773, from Cross Hall, she expresses her concern with Wesley's definition of sin as a voluntary transgression of a known moral law and with any language that hinted at sinless perfection.

At his request, she composed an account of her spiritual experience in which she unhesitatingly reminds him that she was less than impressed the first time she heard him preach but that he had used one particular phrase that kept resounding in her mind and heart: "If it be possible for God to give us a little love, is it not possible for him to fill us with love?"[113] Intrigued and longing for this Christian perfection, she found that this question became fundamental to her spiritual journey and an integral part of her narrative, leading her to an experience of sanctification and, eventually, to her ongoing preaching ministry.

The Public Ministry and Preaching of Mary Bosanquet

Mary Bosanquet's ministry of preaching, meeting with classes, and educating young girls continued in Yorkshire, and though she found herself constantly in debt and her health suffered, her faith sustained her and gave her the boldness to carry on. In early 1773 she was advised to spend some time at Harrogate in hopes of regaining her health. The inn where she resided was filled with noisy people, and their swearing and laughing made her stay in her room as much as possible. She was then asked to hold a prayer meeting at a private home a short distance from Harrogate, and despite her fear of threats, she did so. Not only did some of the main objectors find their hearts touched by her words, but they also informed her fellow guests at the inn; and to her great surprise, they invited her to meet with them in the great ballroom.

Fearful that this would not go well, she nevertheless spoke with them out of concern for their souls, and they met on that day and the following Sunday, and she reported feeling the presence of the Lord in their midst. Shortly afterward, she returned home feeling more at ease in her mind and better in bodily health. She vowed to endeavor to be used by God, even in uncomfortable or unconventional circumstances, trusting in divine strength rather than her own.[114]

Her journal details various ongoing struggles with faith, her continual weakness and illness, and her diffidence at speaking publicly, always affirming that her sense of God's presence in those times of trial and the fruit of her ministry sustained her. Frequently as she visited the sick and met with the children in the places to which she traveled, the people told her that her presence and her words had blessed them. Despite those experiences and affirmations that God indeed owned her work, she felt herself "held in bondage about speaking in public," and after being criticized as an "impudent woman," she set aside May 28, 1775, for prayer and discernment, listing various reasons why preaching publicly was such a cross to her, exclaiming, "Ah, how glad would nature be to find out,—Thou, Lord, dost not require it." Her words echo John Wesley's journal entry of September 6, 1772: "To this day, field preaching is a cross to me. But I know my commission and see no other way of 'preaching the gospel to every creature.'"[115] Like Wesley, she pressed on, obedient to her call.

In September 1775, as she met with a society for the covenant renewal service, it became obvious that she was going to have to exercise her leadership to reprove some of the members for the "little touches of enthusiasm" that had crept in, and she felt unworthy of such a role. Wisely, she prayed about this, recognizing that it would take much wisdom and much love to extinguish false fire and to rekindle the true flame of faith.[116] As she traveled through Huddersfield en route to a meeting in Goker, a friend invited her to stay with her and hold a meeting there upon her return, and Mary agreed. The day was very hot, and the Goker meeting of two or three thousand people was held in a quarry. Some mischievous individuals rolled stones toward the gathered Methodists, but no one was injured, and people were hungry for more and more of her words.

Exhausted, she set off toward Huddersfield but was warned that there were opponents to women's preaching who might cause more trouble. With typical reliance on guidance from God, Mary boldly responded, "If I have a word to speak from Him, He will make my way. If not, the door will be shut. I am only to show the meekness of wisdom and leave all to God." Drained of strength by the heat and the press of bodies, even when the meeting moved outside, Mary stood on a horseblock to preach, her voice clear enough to be heard by all, and at the conclusion, she "felt stronger than when we began."[117]

Reflecting on the ways the hand of the Lord was at work, she later recollected the power of God she had experienced while standing on the horseblock, while also understanding that she must appear ridiculous in the eyes of many people for acting in such a way. In a question-and-answer format similar to her 1771 letter to John Wesley, she muses: "Therefore, if some persons consider me as an impudent woman, and represent me as such, I cannot blame them." When asked why she did not take a round as an itinerant preacher, she responded that her call was different and that she left herself to God's guidance. Pressed to explain why she calls it a "meeting," she says it is more likely to give her full liberty to speak as led, and less likely to offend people. Using a phrase made famous by Wesley, she affirms that while the Quakers indeed have "a good deal of God among them," she believes that

> The Lord is more at work among the Methodists; and while I see this, though they were to toss me about as a football, I would stick to them like a leech. Besides, I do nothing but what Mr. Wesley approves; and as to reproach thrown by some on me, what have I to do with it, but quietly go forward, saying *I will be still more vile*, if my Lord requires it?

Indeed for none but thee, my Lord, would I take up this sore cross. But Thou hast done more for me. . . . Only make me holy, and then lead me as thou wilt.[118]

Though she continued to provide comfort, counsel, and challenge to her Cross Hall family, Mary's financial outlook was dismal, and after rejecting an offer of marriage from a well-to-do neighbor, she began thinking of selling the farm and its stock, dispersing her community, and finding someplace for herself to live. Her thoughts also turned to the Reverend John Fletcher, as a brand-new chapter of life and ministry was about to begin, for her and for her wider circle of friends.[119]

New Directions in Ministry

The Closing of Cross Hall

Overwhelmed by her debts, Mary Bosanquet struggled to discern God's guidance and prayed repeatedly to be shown the way forward. In her journal, she poured out her feelings, noting the many cares that divided her soul and her worry that she might not be able to get the farm and house sold, exclaiming, "It is amazing what losses and trials I have. Yet I feel my anchor cast in the will of God." She astutely and honestly observed that it was easy to believe and trust in God's provision when things were going smoothly, but since all she could see was the probability of financial ruin and the dissolution of her beloved household, it was a real struggle to hold to the promise that God would make a way for each of them.[1]

In this time of trial, her thoughts turned again and again to the Reverend John Fletcher and her concern for his failing health. They had met many years before, and though they held each other in high regard, marriage had never been mentioned, partly because Fletcher did not want anyone to think he was interested in her fortune and partly because at that time Mary felt herself called to a single. She had in fact published a tract in 1766 in the form of an open letter to single Methodist women called *Jesus, Altogether Lovely.* In it, she addresses unmarried women, encouraging them to focus their reading, meditation, and prayer on the advantages of a single life and urging them to remember its privileges. "O cast them not behind you. Nor having beheld the beauties of the lovely Jesus now forget that he is fairer than the sons of men."[2] Nevertheless, she had from time to time wondered if marriage to John Fletcher might be a help rather than a hindrance to her soul.

Jesus, Altogether Lovely was actually written on March 10, 1763, just before Mary Bosanquet and her household settled at Leytonstone, and it is a remarkable document when considered in light of that crucial development in her life and ministry.[3] In the letter, Mary confides to her audience of single women that her desire and prayer for them is that they may "every moment behold Jesus, as *altogether lovely.*" The only way of beholding him, she explains, is by faith, and she seeks to give her readers instructions so they may learn how to keep the eyes of their souls clear, spotless, and flawless like the finest glass. Reminding them that the "grand enemy" cannot hurt them while the eye is simply fixed on Jesus, she warns them that the "roaring lion" will nevertheless continually attack and try to divert their gaze from Jesus, seeking their destruction by presenting various objects to the imagination, sometimes pleasant and sometimes painful. The only remedy lies in self-denial alone. Nothing else will keep the eye of faith clean, and she elaborates on her theme by examining and commending a life that follows a threefold pattern of chastity, poverty, and obedience.[4]

Any deviation from Jesus taken by the soul is understood to be spiritual adultery and a hindrance to the pursuit of the holiness that is the goal, heart, and center of true happiness in God and in life. Accordingly, she advises the women to avoid men, especially those who are single; not to yield to the thought that another way of life might be more advantageous; and to avoid having a spirit of pride or self-righteousness toward others who are not called to this same style of life.[5]

She interprets poverty not as slavish imitation of Christ by giving away all one's possessions but rather in exercising good stewardship over things in whatever sphere of life we are called, understanding that everything we possess is actually God's anyway. Material poverty is not enough, however. "But is this poverty in temporal things all which God requires? Surely, no. It is the *poor in spirit* our Lord hath pronounced blessed, and declares, that theirs is the kingdom of heaven." Reflecting on the text (Matthew 11:29) "Learn of me to be meek and lowly, and ye shall find rest to your souls," she defines poverty of spirit and its fruits as "*true* knowledge of ourselves, from the light of God shining on our hearts, by faith. And this knowledge is the ground and foundation of all religion."[6]

Like her spiritual friend John Wesley, Mary also provides direct, practical counsel on how to endeavor to lead such a life, encouraging her female readers to eschew the trappings and ornaments of ribbons or fancy trimmings on their clothing. Furthermore, she encourages them to avoid becoming the center of attention, never to speak on subjects on which they are ill-informed, and to guard against proud thoughts, self-sufficiency, and "independency of spirit."[7] Following these guidelines, she writes, leads to obedience and humility and to seeing God as all in all.

In Mary's understanding, obedience to God in all things, great and small, necessarily implies self-denial. She points to the necessity of seeing God in everything and "recollecting ourselves in the presence of God, . . . offering up every action to him," for this is the "spirit and life of true religion."[8] This is part and parcel of constantly remembering that we are the work of God's own hands, thereby making ourselves ready to be formed into whatever shape God desires.

In examining the question of why we ought to be obedient to God and to those in authority, Mary reflects that obedience should not arise simply from affection or because someone has done something good for us, calling this idolatry rather than obedience. Likewise, we should not obey because the authority figure is very spiritual and therefore nearer to the heart of Christ than other people. Obedience must instead occur out of love for God, obeying a human authority because it is actually God we obey through that person. She turns to the words of an un-named "holy man" for direction and explication of this concept.

> We should be wholly given up to the conduct of him, whom God hath placed over us, in all things (where no sin lies) following his judgment not our own, except in very

particular cases, where his commands actually wound our conscience, in which case we ought to say so, and lay it before two or three impartial persons. And if they all agree, and we still can't follow his advice it argues not strength but weakness of grace.[9]

Mary enumerates three levels of obedience first described by the nameless author. The lowest degree is to willingly submit to commands we are required to submit to. The second is to comply with orders that we are not obliged to follow, and the third and highest degree of obedience lies in knowing what our superior wishes and doing that person's will without waiting to be ordered to do so.[10] These persons whom we are to obey are the powers "ordained of God," including the leaders of one's country, those in authority in the church, and the authorities within one's family. Again, she stresses that we are bound by God's laws to obey these only as far as we can obey them without sin, and she emphatically declares that we should especially obey "those who watch over our souls."[11]

Mary then summarizes the main points of the letter with a heartfelt cry for her readers to pray for a humble, obedient, and peaceful spirit and to be completely saturated with genuine humility. She adjures them to refrain from setting themselves up as judges of other people who condemn the innocent and excuse the guilty. Mixing allusions from Isaiah 60:18 and Revelation 2:1, Mary exults that if "our spirits [are] humbled in the dust before him . . . then he who still walketh in the midst of the golden candlesticks, and holdeth the stars in his right hand, will be unto us a wall of salvation and our gates shall be praise."[12] She reiterates that her heart's deepest desire is for the reader to abide in faith and endure to the end, holding out the scriptural promise of God's protection and presence, concluding with this joyous statement of trust: "Then will the eternal God be your refuge, and underneath you, the everlasting arms. He will set your sins far from you; and cause you to dwell in purity of heart and in safety. You shall be a people saved of the Lord, who shall himself become your guide and your exceeding great reward."[13]

This model of community laid out by Mary Bosanquet was one of humility. As she planned for the creation of her household with its orphanage and school, she envisioned a Christian life lived in community and rooted in a desire for holiness and happiness that was fleshed out by putting on the virtues of poverty, chastity, and obedience. All her endeavors at establishing a new kind of family, including the difficult last attempt in Yorkshire, were undertaken in that same spirit, and her ministry within her little community and beyond it continued despite her difficulties.

Visiting Bath in February 1778, she attended the laying of the cornerstone for a chapel there by John Wesley. At a love feast that night, she felt led to speak freely, writing in her journal, "Several came to me, one after another, and the Lord's hand hath been with us of a truth. . . . In the classes and bands also, I find much freedom in speaking for God; and He gives me to cast all my own burden on Himself, and to believe, Christ charges himself with all my concerns."[14] Despite ongoing feelings of unworthiness, she continued to speak at various societies and to fast and pray for an answer to her seemingly intractable financial problems.

John Fletcher was brought to mind again during this time of trial. He had never been robustly healthy, and Mary was told that as his health declined, he had gone abroad to his home country of Switzerland in hopes of regaining his strength, though it was feared that he would soon die. Alarmed when she heard that he was dying of tuberculosis, Mary prayed fervently for his recovery and eventual return to England, hoping against hope that he would write to her if his regard for her remained the same. Still trying to carry on at Cross Hall despite the many challenges and disappointments, she repeatedly asked God if she was in the right place, and though she still could not see her way clearly, she felt a reassurance in her heart that God would indeed bring her out of the deep waters, and she resolved to wait for the Lord's salvation.[15]

In her mind, this feeling of deliverance was somehow tied to the anniversary of her arrival in Yorkshire. On June 7, 1781, her journal still reads as a recital of dread and of the difficulty of retaining faith, but on the following day, she received a remarkable letter from John

Fletcher. In it, he declared that he had loved her for twenty-five years and that despite the strangeness of sending such a letter after not seeing each other for some fifteen years, he felt that it was the hand of Providence leading him to write. Mary felt this was quite literally the answer to her prayers, and they corresponded for nearly two months before he visited her in Yorkshire, and they decided that it was "the order of God" that they "should become one" but only after her affairs at Cross Hall were settled and her family settled elsewhere.[16] When she expressed her apprehension about coming into their marriage with a burden of debt, Fletcher professed his love eloquently and with a hint of gentle humor:

> So wilt thou keep 2 years from me to bring me some money. Oh Polly. that is a saying more worthy of Change Alley than of the paradise of love. Let me comfort thee a little. If thou lovest me half as much as I do thee, thou wilt think thyself rich. Thou art worth a million: and cannot I be worth thy £5,000?[17]

Endearingly, shortly before their wedding, in a letter dated September 19, 1781, he wrote to tell her that he had just spoken with someone about patching up the vicarage "for the reception of her to whom I would open heaven if I were the Porter."[18] Accordingly, they were married November 12, 1781, selling most of her furniture with the house and then settling in Madeley, Shropshire, where Fletcher had already been the rector for many years.

Marriage: Friendship and Partnership

Though her marriage and the selling of Cross Hall meant the end of the little community over which Mary had been "mother," it did not end her relationships with the women of her circle but rather enlarged their network to include a new non-female member, John Fletcher. Sarah "Sally" Lawrence, the niece of Sarah Ryan, moved with her to Madeley as an adopted daughter, and John Fletcher became grafted into the circle of friendships, granting his wife's dear deceased friend Sarah Ryan equal status with himself, saying that he, Mary, and Sarah formed a "three-fold cord" and promising Mary that he would be all to her that Sarah had been.[19]

This was neither a marriage of convenience nor a starry-eyed rush into matrimony but rather a marriage of partners who very much loved each other. John Fletcher honored and appreciated the many gifts for ministry that Mary exercised and told her that in marrying him she was also marrying his parish.[20] Rejoicing at their union, Fletcher exclaimed, "God has found me a partner, a *sister*, a *wife*, to use St. Paul's language, who is not afraid to face with me the colliers and barmen of my parish, until death part us."[21] He read from Ephesians 5 at their wedding: "Wives, submit yourselves to your husbands," to which Mary interjected "in the Lord." With hearty agreement, he responded, "If I ever wish you to do anything contrary to the Lord's will, resist me with all your might."[22] That would certainly accord with Mary's understanding of the necessity of obedience to authority.

For her part, upon arriving in Madeley in January 1782, Mary confided to her journal: "I have such a husband as is in every thing suited to me. He bears with all my faults and failings in a manner that continually reminds me of that word, 'Love your wives as Christ loved the church.' His constant endeavour is to make me happy; his strongest desire my spiritual growth."[23] Six months later, as she reflected on the changes that had taken place in her life during the past year, she had nothing but praise and thanksgiving to God for her marriage to John Fletcher and the new ministry opportunities, in her words, "the work among souls" opening up to her in Madeley. She wrote, "I have the kindest and tenderest of husbands; so spiritual a man, and so spiritual a union, I never had any adequate conception of. He is every way suited to me—all I could wish."[24]

As a married woman, Mary found that her responsibilities included many familiar duties, albeit in a different setting. She continued to lead classes and bands; she and her husband both preached in the tithe barn, which they outfitted as a simple, unadorned preaching room; they jointly coordinated the educational activities of the Sunday school; and of course they visited the sick. Always the champion of the single life, John Wesley had worried that marriage might render Mary incapable of pursuing her ministry as before, but in a letter of December 9, 1781, he confided to Hester Ann Roe, "I should not have been willing that Miss Bosanquet should have been joined to any other person than Mr. Fletcher; but I trust she may be as useful with him as she was before."[25] He wrote a similar letter to Dorothy Downes and expressed his warm approval in a letter to John Fletcher himself in almost identical words and advising him, "From the first day which you spend together in Madeley I hope you will lay down an exactly regular plan of living, something like that of the happy family at Leytonstone. Let your light shine to all that are round about you. And let Sister Fletcher do as much as she can for God and no more. To His care I commit you both."[26]

His fears must have been allayed, for after hearing them both speak, he remarked, "Fletcher preached an excellent sermon in the morning and Mrs. Fletcher a more excellent sermon in the evening."[27]

Together, John and Mary Fletcher preached in Wales as well as around Shropshire. At the request of Thomas Coke, accompanied by Sally Lawrence, they even traveled to Dublin to preach and meet with the societies there, despite suffering ill health and enduring seasickness. Great interest was stirred, and a great revival followed their visit. Dozens pressed into the French Church of Dublin to hear John Fletcher preach, and when asked why they went to hear him without being able to understand French, the people responded that they went simply to look at John Fletcher since heaven "seemed to beam from his countenance."[28]

Back at home, the Fletchers busied themselves with the usual pastoral care of a parish and with offering hospitality to itinerating ministers. Theirs was very much a joint ministry in which she had the freedom to preach around the regular preaching places of the parish as well as out of doors. Because they realized that a future vicar of the Madeley parish might be less than welcoming to Methodists, they constructed a little chapel that was under Wesley's appointment from 1784 onward.[29]

Not surprisingly, given Mary's experience and expertise, the Fletchers established a school in which they taught religion, reading, and writing to their students, using music as a way of teaching them to read. John Fletcher apparently had a gift for turning the simplest thing into a lesson, using the unexpected arrival of a robin in the classroom as an opportunity to speak to the children of God's love and care for the creatures of the earth.[30]

Mary continued preaching in the tithe barn and speaking elsewhere on Sundays as well as meeting with classes and bands, using a question-and-answer format to connect with her listeners, similar to the outline she used in her letter to Wesley about the extraordinary call.[31] She continued conducting a rigorous self-examination in her journal particularly on her birthday, sometimes questioning her obedience to God's will but always rejoicing in the blessings that came her way. On her forty-third birthday, September 12, 1782, she spent much of the day in quiet reflection and prayer, reporting a feeling of some sorrow and a lack of wisdom, light, and love. However, she contentedly writes, "My spiritual sphere of action is different. I have in many respects a wider call for action than before."[32]

Two years later, on her birthday, she again marvels at the goodness of God, giving thanks for her husband and for the receptivity to her ministry from the Madeley community. "My call is also so clear, and I have such liberty in the work, and such sweet encouragement among the people." In addition, her servant and dearly loved "child," Sally Lawrence, was in better health, and financial worries were a thing of the past. "An income quite comfortable, and a good deal to help the poor with. O what shall I render to the Lord, for all the mercies he hath shown unto me."[33]

In his book *More About Early Methodist People*, Leslie Church fulsomely commends her for her "winsome personality, her self-effacing benevolence, and her splendid courage in face of the most severe opposition" and remarks that these characteristics combined to appeal to the many individuals and congregations who flocked to hear her preach. "Hers was no ordinary call but was so surely a divine vocation that to have denied it because of a human regulation would have been little short of blasphemy."[34]

Widowhood: Continuation of Ministry at Madeley

Both Mary and John Fletcher experienced a great deal of illness, yet they carried on their ministry while suffering pain, fever, and other physical woes. Sadly, on August 14, 1785, John Fletcher breathed his last, ending what had been a successful co-pastorate in all but name.[35] Of his death, the grief-stricken Mary recorded in her journal, "The sun of my earthly joys forever set, and the cloud arose which casts the sable on all my future life. . . . In former parts of my life, I have felt deep sorrow; but such were now my feelings, that no words that I am able to think of can convey an adequate idea thereof."[36]

To add to her sorrow, a rumor reached her that a story was spreading about John Fletcher's death, insinuating that his faith faltered at the end and that he had suffered great agony and delirium. Methodists put great stock in "dying well" with confidence and joy, so this was a particularly hurtful story. Even as a brand-new widow, she could not let things lie, and she ably took pen in hand to set the matter straight.

To refute these unkind allegations, she composed a lengthy letter to John Wesley on August 18, 1785, describing not only her husband's last moments but the last few days of his life and his utter calm acceptance of his approaching death. She wrote that even when his speech had begun to fail, he was moved to say that "God is love, love, love" and that his visage was so composed and even triumphant that it was hard to see a change once death had come. She concluded this letter by pointing out in sorrowful detail that they had only been married three years, nine months, and two days, telling Wesley that her soul was filled with anguish that could only be consoled by abandoning herself to the will of God and looking toward being reunited in the life to come.[37] To cope with her grief, she threw herself wholeheartedly back into her ministry of meeting with the people of the parish and dedicating herself to prayer.

With the death of her husband, Mary not only suffered the loss of her partner and companion; she faced the very real likelihood of losing her home and ministerial base in Madeley. She began to worry about where to go next, remembering that John Fletcher had advised her to stay in the area where she was settled and respected and usefully employed in ministry. Seeking to know God's will in the matter, she prayed and read the Bible and finally felt able to adjust to a new life elsewhere if necessary. Wesley urged her to move to London, but she came to believe that her place was still in Madeley.

To Mary's great delight, the new vicar told her that she could remain in the same house, renting it for as long as she liked. She found herself wielding a great deal of influence and authority as a result. Because she knew the people and needs of the parish so well, it was arranged that the curate appointed for the pastoral work and celebrating the sacraments would always be cleared with her first.[38] Additionally, the title deed of the tithe barn, also known as the Madeley Barn Methodist chapel, was in her name, and she nominated the trustees. She dominated the Church of England and Methodist religious life of the parish of Madeley for thirty years.[39]

Mary continued preaching and meeting with people in Madeley and beyond, preaching as many as five times a week in the tithe barn.[40] From the time of John Fletcher's death in 1785 until her own death in 1815, she served as the incumbent pastor of Madeley in all but name, preaching, catechizing, meeting with societies and classes, and caring for the temporal as well as spiritual needs of the community. She was so beloved that the people would have fiercely resisted any efforts to remove or replace her, and she was devoted to the Church of England as well as the Methodist movement, lamenting the growing friction between the two. Her adopted daughters Sally Lawrence and, later, Mary Tooth assisted her in her ministry, praying publicly, leading classes, exhorting, and preaching.[41] The situation in Madeley was harmonious until the arrival of a new curate, Samuel Walter, in 1792.

Saddened that Walter had publicly expressed a desire for the Methodists to separate and a division to be made between them and the parish church, she appealed to Walter by equating her late husband with Elijah and Walter with Elisha, praying that a double portion of Fletcher's "dovelike spirit" would fall upon Walter.[42] In many kind but direct letters, she argued for the continued unity of the parish church and Methodists. She apparently convinced him, and for the next twenty-one years he worked jointly with her.[43] Remarkably and significantly, she even took on some of the liturgical worship leadership in the parish church on occasion. On Monday, December 21, 1795, she wrote in her journal about her activities at the Sunday service on the preceding day. Because Mr. Walter was away, she "had to meet the congregation. For an hour and three quarters I felt much freedom, and some life in speaking, singing, and prayer."[44]

Her adopted daughter and dear companion Mary Tooth recorded at least two other such occasions. On one, Mary Fletcher read the psalms and scripture lessons for the day and preached from Genesis 28; and on another occasion, she expounded on John 6, taking Mr. Walter's place when he became ill.[45] Thus, at a time when most Methodists were being forced out of their parish churches across England, the Methodists and the congregation of the parish church in Madeley remained blended in one fellowship, largely due to the influential efforts of Mary Bosanquet Fletcher, but this unity did not long survive after her death in 1815.[46]

Journal entries written a few months before her death reveal her awareness and her anguish at the prospect of disunity.

> We have had for thirty years a oneness among our people;—but now there is a division, by the desire of the minister. . . . But I here declare, I have been joined to the people united to Mr. Wesley for above threescore years, and I trust to die among them. . . . I have always considered myself as a member of the church, and so have the united friends in Madeley. In some measure we are now pushed out. . . . The church minister has repeatedly expressed a wish that the Methodists should be a separate people; as he always thought it best for the church people, and the people called Methodists, to move in distinct lines.[47]

Mary Fletcher's Meetings

One of the many people converted under Mary Fletcher's preaching was a man named William Tranter, who became a Methodist minister himself. His description of her meetings, published in the *Methodist Magazine* in 1837, clearly illustrates her own considerable efforts to promote unity between the Methodist society and the parish church by maintaining a rhythm of worship that incorporated both: "On the Sabbath, the pious people, . . . usually arrived in time for Mrs. Fletcher's morning meeting. The religious services for the day were as follows: after prayer, with which the service always commenced, a beautiful, prepared piece, called 'The Watchword,' was read."[48]

Mary Fletcher's influence was so widespread partly because of her voluminous correspondence with hundreds of women and men who looked upon her as a "Mother in Israel," and they thought nothing of making long journeys to see and hear her preach.[49] Through her letters, she is seen as "authoritative, informative, and occasionally peremptory" in a time of increasing official resistance to female preaching and other public activity.[50] Through her correspondence, she provided spiritual counsel and encouragement as well as reproofs, and she was a mentor and example to many of the other female preachers, including Mary Barritt (later Taft) as well as to her companions Sarah Lawrence and Mary Tooth.

At her Sunday meetings, after the preaching service, she would speak to the aged among them who had traveled a great distance, advising, encouraging, and if needed, admonishing them. She also invited any strangers in attendance to share their religious experience, an activity at which she excelled. Afterward, "the chiming of the church going bell was then heard, and the assembly separated to meet again in the parish church close at hand, to which the people very generally repaired. Mrs. Fletcher always, if in health."[51]

At noon, visitors and the poor who had not brought food from home were invited to dine with Mary Fletcher at her home or ate at the local inn before attending her one o'clock meeting, which lasted until the bell for the afternoon service at the parish church. During the course of her meetings, "she read the life of some eminently holy person" and made discerning "remarks of her own on the excellency or defects of the character" of the person.[52]

Mary Fletcher's Preaching Style

Her own sermons and meditations were carefully designed discourses with a distinctive Methodist accent, based on scripture and showing an awareness of the realities of life in the Madeley parish. The germ for what grew into her "watchwords" began to stir in her mind after a conversation with a parishioner who reminisced about a series of sermons preached by John Fletcher in which he examined the titles given to Christ in the Bible. Though she searched for any notes her husband might have left behind, she found none; however, this conversation stimulated her to try her hand at something similar.[53]

According to Mary Tooth, this process began in July 1797:

[She] has begun to give the society a watchword for the ensuing fortnight. The first was Adam Cor. 15 v. 45. The last fortnight it was Advocate (1 John 2 v.1). Tonight's was Alpha and Omega, the beginner and the finisher. Rev. 1. v.3. Heb. 12. v.2. The circumstance that led to her doing so was this, Mr Hughes one day mentioned that Mr Fletcher at one time took the name of our Lord, and afterwards of the Church, and preached from them, but was not able to give her anything of the substance of them it was pressed upon her mind to write a few lines on each and entitle it a watchword.[54]

These "watchwords" were short discourses based on the various names of Christ and of the church, which Mary Fletcher and Mary Tooth lightly edited and revised repeatedly for at least thirty years with an eye toward publication. Based on texts from the Bible, the watchwords represent an important component of her preaching ministry, informed by her years of experience as a preacher and teacher from the time of her residence at Leytonstone and Cross Hall. The inspiration may have come from her husband's example, but the manner of her exposition of the biblical texts did not simply mimic the sermonic conventions of her day but was a core element of her own particular "empathic religiosity."[55]

Mary Fletcher preached either without notes or with notes written on scraps of paper to be at hand should she require them.[56] She organized the "watchwords" in numbered "heads" that could be elaborated upon as needed, preaching them alphabetically and focusing on a single attribute or name for Christ each week. The "watchwords" were received with great enthusiasm as she recounted and embroidered upon familiar biblical stories and images while urging her listeners to listen with their hearts and to open themselves emotionally to God.[57] The "watchwords" stand as the crowning achievement of Mary Fletcher's written legacy; and as devotional literature, their spiritual insight is the equal of any of her contemporaries. Their simplicity and clarity of expression make them "more accessible to the modern reader than the published sermons of either John or Charles Wesley."[58]

Phyllis Mack and David Wilson point out that the lyricism of Mary's sermons and devotional writings do indeed make them more accessible than the writings of either Wesley brother or of her own husband John Fletcher, but they also point to at least two other obvious differences. Mary Fletcher's writings exhibit an absence of "rhetorical violence" in which human sinfulness is portrayed in dramatic and even morbid terms as in a sermon by Charles Wesley on John 8:1-11, which urges his "stiff-necked and uncircumcised in heart and ears" listeners to hear his words and tremble lest they die in their iniquity. She infrequently employed threats of damnation or hurled accusations, more often pointing out the trivial everyday habits that cause ordinary people to be inattentive to God, diverting them from love of God and neighbor and leading inexorably to more egregious sins.[59] As well, she sometimes employed a question-and-answer, conversational format that encouraged discussion rather than passive listening.[60]

In addition, the "you" Mary Fletcher addressed in her sermons was typically the "individual, vulnerable fellow seeker" rather than the collective assembly of gathered sinners, and she frequently used the first-person "we," thereby avoiding any hint of condescension toward her congregation since she included herself as well. Similar to William Law and John Wesley, she attempted to cultivate self-awareness by illuminating the ways the common preoccupations of life gradually wear away the soul's integrity and inculcate full-blown sins.[61] She would certainly have affirmed the sentiments of Susanna Wesley as expressed in a letter to John dated July 8, 1725: "Whatever weakens your reason, impairs the tenderness of your conscience, obscures your sense of God, takes off your relish for spiritual things, whatever increases the authority of the body over the mind, that thing is sin to you, however innocent it may seem in itself."[62]

Mary Fletcher's "Watchwords"

By publicly linking her "watchwords" with her late husband's sermons, Mary cleverly established the validity of her public speech in the face of ongoing controversy over the practice of female preaching. At the same time, she made it clear that the watchwords were her own original work, used week in and week out in the meetings of the Madeley Methodists. Some of the "watchwords" are in question-and-answer form, most likely for use in class meetings, though by their very nature they were flexible enough to suit various occasions. Intended for publication, they were passed over during the early nineteenth century and disregarded, probably because they were seen as sermons even though they were not described as such.[63] For that reason, it is worthwhile to examine them at some length since they not only represent the mature spiritual thought and preaching of Mary Fletcher herself but in some sense stand for the lost writings and sermons of so many of her sister preachers.

Watchword: Eagle

The wide range of imagery Mary Fletcher employs in her "watchwords" is striking and noteworthy since so little from the pen of early Methodist female preachers remains preserved in the historical record. For example, her "watchword" for the word "eagle," based on Deuteronomy 32:11, focuses on the maternal imagery of God as a mother bird whose nurturing invites her young to eschew the worldly delights found in the nest in favor of taking flight and detaching from them.[64] Perhaps this imagery is not surprising, given that she had experienced a powerful vision of herself as a nursing mother who was tenderly feeding God's children.

Phrase by phrase, she draws on other scripture passages to explicate her message. Her use of Old Testament imagery of Exodus and the New Testament accounts of Christ weeping over Jerusalem paints a vivid picture of a mothering Savior who feeds her young, bears them on wings of love, and protects them from harm.

Mary Fletcher does not simply draw from the richness of scripture in her meditation upon the eagle. She also extracts lines from Charles Wesley's Communion hymn "Come, Sinners to the Gospel Feast" to emphasize the universal nature of God's love and care, the gift offered to all people everywhere and not just to some elect few: "How often hath he spread his arms wide open to our souls, while he impressed with power those words on our hearts:

> Ye need not one be left behind
> For God hath bidden all mankind."

Adding a verse from another of Charles Wesley's hymns, she further extols the saving grace of the One who is mediator and savior, who is like the mother eagle who puts herself between her young ones and danger, interposing herself between the archer and her beloved young whom she bears to safety upon her wings:

> My peace is made,
> My ransom is paid,
> My soul on thy bloody atonement is stay'd.[65]

Drawing from Hebrews and Psalms, Mary Fletcher further unfolds her reflections on this eagle metaphor. She describes the perfect obedience of Christ as seen in his bearing us up before God's throne, in paying our debt, and in doing our work, carrying us through our trials and temptations, carrying us through both fire and water, preparing us for our eternal place with God, "becoming the finisher as well as the author of our faith" (Hebrews 12:2). Concluding with an allusion to Isaiah 63, she exclaims that it is as if Jesus cries out that he alone bears our burdens and treads the winepress, having no one to share in his sufferings and that he therefore asks that we not share our affections with another but instead turn our eyes only toward him.[66]

Watchword: Babe

From regarding the Godhead as a mother eagle, Mary extends this maternal image to Jesus himself. In her explication of the title of "babe" with regard to Christ, she not only reflects upon the infant Jesus but also turns the metaphor on its head to depict him as a mother to his children in the church.[67] After describing the glory that Jesus left in order to take on our nature and thereby restore us to God, she remarks, "And while we look on Jesus in his childhood, how should it encourage us to pray for that posture of soul, which the Lord hath pronounced to be the only entrance into communion with God." This leads her to muse upon the words of Christ in which he said that entrance into the kingdom of heaven was for those who outwardly become as little children, fully trusting in God for everything.

> But the outward helplessness and weakness of a babe is a fine figure of what we ought to be. The child has no care: it leaves all to its nurse and has no thought for tomorrow. It takes food for poison just as you give it. It has a perfect confidence in its mother, and, in her bosom, its self, secure, though surrounded with real danger. And this is the state of a soul fully born of God and renewed after his image. It is centered in his will and rests secure. . . .
>
> The expressions of babe or child are often repeated in scripture; as if the Holy Spirit took a singular pleasure in pointing us to that strange instance of love and humility, as the very model of our imitation, and the source of our greatest comfort.[68]

Mary briefly returns to this striking image of Jesus as our mother in her reflections on his title of "bridegroom." As she examines Matthew 9:15, she observes:

Sometimes the church is addressed and invited as a babe to its mother; then as a son whom his Father loves; but in this and many other places: as a bride adorned for the bridegroom. For by taking that title, our blessed Lord gives the strongest assurance, he will make her so. Well then, poor soul, what hast thou to fear? Jesus will nurse thee as a babe; teach thee as a son; and prepare thee for his bosom—yes, the very delight of his soul.[69]

This interest in and emphasis on the maternal nature of Christ was not wholly without precedent within the wider history of Christianity—some of the "showings" of Julian of Norwich in the fourteenth century led her to refer to Christ as our true Mother, nor was it unknown even within Methodism—but it was somewhat unusual in its directness. While Charles Wesley nowhere explicitly uses the name "mother" for God or Christ in his hymns, he compares the tenderness of a mother for a child to the love of Christ in "A Hymn for Love,"

Ask if a mother's heart is kind
To her own sucking child,
Then ask, is God to love inclin'd,
Or my Redeemer mild?

A mother may perhaps neglect,
And her own son forget,
But Jesus never will reject
A sinner at his feet.[70]

Another of his hymns, "Congratulations to a Friend, Upon Believing in Christ," also echoes the language of God as the mother eagle feeding her young and bearing them aloft with her wings,

And will he now forsake His own
Or lose the purchase of His blood?
No, for He looks with pity down
He watches over thee for good;
Gracious He eyes thee from above,

And guards and feeds thee with His Love. . . .

Still may His love thy fortress be,
And make thee still His darling care,
Settle, confirm, and stablish thee,
On eagle's wings thy spirit bear:
Fill thee with heaven and ever shed
His choicest blessings on thy head.[71]

While some scholars have construed Charles Wesley's frequent references to the sinner hiding in the bleeding side wound of the crucified Christ as unconsciously reflecting sexual desire, Mack asserts that they might better be interpreted as a desire for maternal protection and power and a reminder that the Christian's safety lay in total dependence upon God.[72] For example, in the early hymn "Where Shall My Wondering Soul Begin?", Charles Wesley points to Christ's embrace and parental welcome:

His bleeding heart shall make you room;
His open side shall take you in;
He calls you now, invites you home;
Come, O my guilty brethren, come.[73]

Watchword: Door

Mary Fletcher beautifully explores and expands theologically upon the "I am" sayings of Jesus taken from John 10, particularly the verse in which he calls himself the gate or, in her words, the door. She lists several ways in which Jesus is the door to pardon, holiness, and blessing, emphasizing his acts of taking our debt as his own and putting his own spirit within us, imparting that spirit of holiness to all in order to save "unto the uttermost" everyone who comes to God the Father through him. His work includes healing our infirmities, conveying every rich blessing to us through the channel of his blood, and offering peace and rest to everyone who is weary and heavy-laden, as recorded in the gospel of Matthew.[74]

This door is always open to sinners, and the only key to the door is the key of faith. Mary Fletcher urges everyone not to hesitate but to cast body and soul on Jesus's love, resting and living confidently into the words from the Lord's Prayer, "thy will be done." Those who enter through the door will experience particular rewards or advantages; namely, they shall be saved, dwelling secure in every danger they encounter, entering and exiting freely, finding pasture in the safety of the Lord who shields, feeds, and waters them, bestowing upon them the gift of everlasting life.[75]

Watchword: Shepherd

Her treatment of the beloved image of Christ as the Good Shepherd in John 10 provides one final illustration of her gift for taking familiar scripture and interpreting it through a Wesleyan Methodist lens in order to share the gospel in a unique but easily understandable way. In doing so, she is following the divine example of a loving God who utilizes every possible means of reaching and stirring up the unknowing and ignorant hearts of humankind.

> So stupid and dull is the heart of man, he hath need of every method to be followed, that can awaken up his spiritual senses. Therefore, the God of love, in condescension to our weakness, hath made choice of the most familiar terms, to describe the near relation, which subsists between himself and the soul of man. One of which is that of shepherd.[76]

Mary Fletcher states that God's great truth was revealed to David by faith, inspiring him to compose Psalm 23 with its familiar imagery of the Lord as shepherd. Turning to John 10, she compares the two passages in order to show that Jesus is the Good Shepherd spoken of in the Twenty-third Psalm. In John 10, Jesus tells us repeatedly that he is our shepherd, an important title that implies certain responsibilities and duties exercised on behalf of the sheep and lambs he tends. Linking this comforting Old Testament image with the New Testament understanding of Christ the Savior, she elaborates on these important obligations to be fulfilled by a conscientious herder of sheep.

It is the duty of a shepherd to watch over his flock and to guard them from all enemies.

The common enemies of sheep may be slain with a weapon; but our grand adversary, eternal condemnation, could be no way conquered, but by the death of the good shepherd. Therefore, says he, *I am the good shepherd, I lay down my life for the sheep.* But the shepherd leads them to pasture, covers them from the heat, and cleans them from all defilement. So the saviour is himself the shadow, which screens from the heat of justice; and his blood cleanses from all sin, and causes their robes to be completely white, who wash therein.[77]

The way she draws parallels and inferences from other biblical texts into her sermon and examines the context in which the scripture was written is indicative of her use of study materials and commentaries. Most often these included the books John Wesley recommended in his course of study for women, as well as resources from the well-stocked library of her late husband, but Mary also relies upon firsthand knowledge and experience in illustrating many of her points. Having lived on a Yorkshire farm for years, she was well acquainted with the habits of shepherds and sheep, and she knowledgeably contrasts the contemporary method of herding flocks with the first-century way of tending them. Whereas sheep in rural England would be gathered and driven by a shepherd, possibly with canine assistance, it was different in Jesus's day.

I observed, he led them to pasture; the words are, *He calls his own sheep by name and leadeth them out*: an allusion to the eastern shepherds, who did not drive their sheep as we do, but walked before them, and, by a particular call, the flock were accustomed to follow. So our true shepherd goes before us in every way, wherein we are called to go. [12] He suffered all manner of reproaches, grief and sorrows, and hath left us an example that we should tread in his steps. He hath passed through death before us, and taken away the sting; yea he hath risen again, the first fruit of them that slept, and he will present himself to every danger, so that, by keeping close behind him, no enemy can strike us, unless the weapon could enter through him, who is our impenetrable shield. On this account he says, Follow me for he that followeth me shall not walk in darkness.[78]

She deftly weaves together the threads connecting the title of shepherd of Psalm 23 and of John 10 together, demonstrating a close familiarity with the Bible by almost unconsciously drawing upon additional passages from Isaiah 40, Isaiah 43, Luke 12, and Matthew 10.

> But *he calleth his own sheep by name*, not only with the general call, which moved the whole flock, but he calls each by their name. *I have*, says he (by the prophet), *called thee by thy name*. I have surnamed thee, though thou didst not know me; and by his own voice he tells us, *I know my sheep, and am known of mine*. Yes every, the most feeble, believer, is noted in his book; the hairs of his head are all numbered by him, who holds the seas in his right hand. He, even he who rules with the strong hand of a prince, leads and feeds with the kind hand of a shepherd. His word is the food for them to feed on—and his ordinances are the field for them to feed in, and he promises they shall go in and out and find pasture.

For Mary Fletcher, hearing God's voice and rejecting the enticements of a stranger is not simply a matter of knowing Christ and hearing God's word in scripture and then choosing not to be disobedient. Just as Wesley emphasized the importance of both inner and outer holiness, Mary witnesses to that same understanding. The Christian who is striving to be made holy is not interested in just outward obedience or lip service but a real change within, a constant sense of being attuned to the Holy Spirit, which develops in the heart by recognizing and responding to the voice of the shepherd and rejecting the stranger's allurements.

> But surely it goes much further. Can it imply less than a constant inward attention to the teaching of the spirit, a continual uniting of the powers of the soul, by faith to God, and a

faithful rejection of those unprofitable, and hurtful thoughts, which Satan is ever striving to thrust in? Yea the true and watchful sheep will flee from these thoughts, as from the face of a serpent: they know not the voice of this stranger.[79]

Studying the works of Mary Bosanquet Fletcher has been critical, but what were other Methodist female preachers and leaders doing in the late eighteenth and early nineteenth century?

The "Female Brethren"

Following the closure of Cross Hall and the marriage of Mary Bosanquet and John Fletcher, a number of female preachers, including Sarah Crosby and Ann Tripp, created a new community and support system in Yorkshire. This family of Methodist women settled in a small house near the Boggard House, the parent Methodist chapel of Leeds, where Sarah Crosby headed up the group of women preachers and class leaders who named themselves with no sense of conscious irony, the "Female Brethren."[80] It is likely that they chose this designation to indicate their strong sense of unity and spiritual purpose, appropriating masculine language because, unlike the "brethren" within Methodism, a group of Methodist sisters had no readily available identity, as the correlated term "sistren" had fallen out of use after the sixteenth century.[81] Use of the term "Female Brethren" was therefore a way of clearly denoting their prominence, fellowship, and oneness in Christ, a reality that was undeniably true even after Wesley's death.

Despite never being officially sanctioned and appointed as itinerants by the Methodist Conference, these "Female Brethren" preached and traveled extensively throughout Yorkshire, around Manchester, and even into London. Their community was created to provide support and encouragement for the preaching women of the Methodist revival through Christian conferencing, meeting in bands or classes, studying scripture together, tending the needs of the poor of the community, and offering counsel and guidance through the frequent exchange of letters.

Even without official standing, these "Female Brethren" exerted a substantial degree of influence within Methodism, even with John Wesley. In 1789, Conference met in Leeds, and it was decided that Adam Clarke, a prominent minister and scholar, would be stationed in the Leeds Circuit. The stewards of the Circuit had petitioned Wesley to send Clarke there, and he had drawn large crowds who came to hear him preach in July at Conference.[82] In 1788, Clarke was married to Mary Cooke, one of Wesley's frequent correspondents. Wesley valued her piety and abilities highly and had asked Adam Clarke in a letter dated November 5, 1788, to encourage her to exercise her gifts in pastoral care and spiritual counsel as a "deaconess." Despite all this, Ann Tripp, Sarah Crosby, and the other "Female Brethren" protested against his appointment. It is not clear why they were averse to his being stationed there, as he was outwardly supportive of their work; nevertheless, though Wesley reserved the right to appoint the itinerants where he thought best, he yielded to their wishes and stationed Clarke in the Halifax Circuit instead.

However, the women of the Halifax Circuit found Clarke no more acceptable than the "Female Brethren" had and argued against him being stationed there. Their objections were not because they disliked Clarke or found his theology or character questionable but because, as they said, "Though Dr. Clarke was learned, . . . he was dull." Wesley acquiesced and wound up sending Clarke to the Bristol Circuit.[83] Clarke rather huffily replied that he did not think his call extended to any place where women were the "governors" and that it was certainly not Christ's intentions for women to hold the reins.[84]

The "Female Brethren" sought sanctification and a deeper sense of inner holiness throughout their lives, and Sarah Crosby found that her intense experiences of God's presence made her long for that holiness more and more. Her life was a model of the Wesleyan understanding of Christian perfection as a dynamic progression toward God in which she was an active participant.

Suffering from rheumatism, Sarah traveled less as she grew older. As she reflected on her life and her career as a preacher and leader, she confided to her journal, "I am now near seventy. . . . I am often afflicted with painful infirmities of body, and I am not altogether without temptation of different kinds, though I am assaulted with few, very few, that interrupt my peace. . . . I live by faith in Jesus my precious Saviour, and find my last are my best days, not one of all the good things the Lord hath promised having failed."[85]

Rejoicing in God's faithfulness in preserving her life and for blessing her ministry, she wrote of her insatiable desire for more of God's Spirit: "I have enjoyed many reviving seasons for these last few months, blessed be my Lord. But I long for deeper manifestations of the divine nature. O, when shall I be overwhelmed with thy delightful presence."[86]

Death of Sarah Crosby

Sarah Crosby continued to faithfully serve the Lord up to the end of her life, devoting herself to the gospel through writing letters of spiritual counsel, preaching, and meeting with classes of thirty people apiece twice a week as well as with bands. She rejoiced that many of those whom she had mentored and guided in their discipleship kept in contact with her through their letters and that some were even able to visit and worship with her.[87] A few years before her death, she wrote a letter to Frances Mortimer Pawson, whom she had befriended and mentored. In it, she apologizes for not writing more often, citing ill health, particularly rheumatic pain, but she cheerfully praises God: "But glory be to God, I believe all things shall work together for good. So my mind is supported and I go comfortably on through pain . . . living the present moment in prayer and praise. Labour is rest, and pain is ease, whilst thou my Lord art here."[88]

Sarah Crosby's story offers insight into the experience of Christian perfection as the narrative of one woman's life as a Methodist preacher and leader. She shares with her readers the joy of conversion and the way in which honest soul-searching reveals the ongoing presence of sin and, more importantly, the ways in which faith in God's transforming love released her from the grip of that inbred sin. In her words, we see a great passion for loving others and bearing witness to them about God's love for her, for them, and for all people, and she clearly describes the deep yearning for more of

God that resulted from each experience of being in the divine presence.[89] Passionate love of God and concern for others remained with her until the very end, and in one of her final letters, she wrote to her friend Elizabeth Ritchie Mortimer that she had received the assurance from God: "I will never leave thee."[90]

Sarah's friend and companion, Ann Tripp, kept a record of the last days before Sarah's death on October 29, 1804, and it was a witness to dying well, which was an important confirmation of faith among Methodists. Her "good death" is illustrative of the dedication and devotion of this beloved "Mother in Israel." Despite being ill and weak, Sarah met with two classes and testified at a select band gathering in the days prior to her death; and on Sunday, just one day before she died, she attended a 7:00 a.m. worship service, a society meeting, and evening services.[91] A much shortened and edited version of this account would finally be published in the *Methodist Magazine* after much agitating from Ann Tripp and Elizabeth Ritchie Mortimer, and Zechariah Taft included excerpts from Sarah Crosby's diaries and the account of her death in his *Biographical Sketches of Holy Women.*[92] Taft held Sarah Crosby in high regard and glowingly acknowledged her in his sketch of her life and ministry as "an apostolic woman" and as "an *itinerant,* yea, a *field preacher.*"[93]

One of the many letters from her longtime friend Elizabeth Ritchie Mortimer to the editor of the *Methodist Magazine* is included by Taft in the second volume of *Holy Women.* Entrusted with Sarah Crosby's papers by Ann Tripp, Elizabeth opens with these words of commendation and respect for Sarah Crosby's life, ministry, and faithful witness, not for herself alone but for many thousands who benefited from her preaching, her spiritual counsel, and her gentle reproof:

> Many have expressed a desire to see an account of that mother in our Israel, Mrs. Crosby. . . . Permit me to add, for near 36 years I have been favoured with the particular friendship of this blessed woman, and for zeal for the glory of God, love to precious souls, manifested by unwearied labours, faithfulness in reproving what she thought wrong, and a happy facility in encouraging souls to struggle up the

hill of holiness, have found few to equal her; but her praise is in all the churches: she lives in the memory of thousands; many who are gathered home have cause to bless God they ever knew her, as well as many who are still engaged in the glorious warfare.[94]

Ann Tripp died in 1823 and was buried alongside her co-laborers in the gospel, Sarah Ryan and Sarah Crosby, in the churchyard of St. Peter's in Leeds. The inscription on the tombstone of these remarkable Methodist women fittingly read:

Here lies the body of
Mrs. SARAH RYAN,
Who departed this life August, 1768, aged 41.
Also of Mrs. SARAH CROSBY,
Who entered with perfect peace into the joy of her Lord,
October 29, 1804; aged 75.
A mother in Israel hath she been, and her works shall
    praise her in the gate.
Beneath this stone is interred the
Body of ANN TRIPP, aged 78 years,
Who departed this life
Sept. 16, 1823.[95]

The Pawsons: Partners in Marriage, Partners in Ministry

While Sarah Crosby and Ann Tripp were at the center of the "Female Brethren," there was a wider network of women connected with them and with Mary Bosanquet Fletcher, a support system that included female preachers and class leaders from across England. Many of these women were never married; some were widowed and remained single; some delayed marriage until later; and some like Frances Mortimer Pawson exercised their ministries alongside their preacher husbands, following the pattern of partnership exemplified by John and Mary Fletcher.

Frances Mortimer

Frances Mortimer was born May 11, 1736, in York into a cultured family of means who insured that she receive an education even after her father's death when she was sixteen.[96] From her journal, considered a classic of Methodist spirituality, it is obvious that she was well-read and intelligent. Among the books mentioned are William Law's *A Serious Call to a Devout and Holy Life*, Thomas à Kempis's *Imitation of the Life of Christ*, and John Wesley's extract of *The Life of De Renty*.[97] Unlike the writings of many other early Methodist women, her work was not consigned to complete oblivion after her death, but nevertheless it was heavily edited by Joseph Sutcliffe, who published her journals as *The Experience of the Late Mrs. Frances Pawson, Widow of the Late Rev. John Pawson*.[98]

For many years, like most women of her social circle, she entertained herself chiefly by reading novels and paying social calls, and her life was devoted to leisure pursuits until she was invited to stay with a newly married friend, Mrs. Nisdale, in London. Mr. Nisdale was a serious man who expected his household to follow a pattern of regular public worship and private family devotions, an expectation that showed her that Christianity could be the focal point of one's life. Upon returning to York, she became determined to reshape her own life along those lines.[99]

For about two years Frances endured bouts of confusion, doubt, and even depression, finding it nearly impossible to develop and maintain a new pattern for her life without the support of serious Christian friends as she tried to "work out her own salvation" more or less on her own. Her journal entries from this period contain earnest phrases like "conscious rectitude" and "endearing self-applause" as she struggled with the difficulty of changing good intentions into action as she tried to take baby steps forward.[100]

Lamenting that she had wasted so much time with tea parties and idle chit-chat, she resolved to reduce the time spent calling on friends. She began changing her habits, reading the Bible instead of novels, and engaging in prayer every morning and evening with her maid at her home. Additionally, she began to attend religious meetings in the home of Mrs. Carr, an Anglican evangelical woman, and she became interested in the ideas and lifestyle of the many Methodists she encountered there.[101]

Involvement with the Methodists

Frances's mother and her brother, the Reverend Charles Mortimer, attempted to dissuade her from becoming involved with this group. Her family, disturbed by her unexpected tendency toward "religious enthusiasm," tried to discourage her newfound zeal, but she was not deterred.[102] The spiritual counsel of John Spence, a leader of a Methodist class in York, helped her resolve some of her inner spiritual turmoil, and Frances continued to hear Methodist preachers, despite worrying about the stigma of being associated with them. Mrs. Carr continued to be influential in her spiritual growth, and momentously, on June 19, 1774, she met Sarah Crosby for the first time, calling her "an eminently pious woman." In her journal she wrote, "She seemed much interested in my welfare, and gave me many instructions, and advised me particularly to pray with simplicity, and to request the Lord to teach me to come to him with all the simplicity of a little child. She desired my good, not only on my own account, but with a view to the good it would prove to others."[103]

They became friends and struck up an epistolary friendship, but Frances found face-to-face conversations with Sarah Crosby much more satisfactory than the exchange of letters. In December 1774, Frances attended a meeting at which Sarah expounded on 1 Corinthians 13, and her words filled Frances with a yearning for the divine love Sarah described so well.

In July of the same year, Frances had heard John Wesley preach, an occasion that impressed her deeply. In her journal she described meeting him: "His venerable looks inspired me with a veneration for him I cannot express. Mrs. Hall invited me to breakfast with him. I accepted the invitation, and was much pleased to see how this great minister of the gospel conducted himself among his preachers, with cheerfulness, ease, and simplicity."[104] Frances also came into Mary Bosanquet Fletcher's orbit, and they began corresponding in 1776. Upon reading a letter from Mary on sanctification, Frances wrote in her journal that "every sentence seemed a portion of meat for my soul and it enlarged my heart in prayer to obtain the blessing."[105]

A budding friendship with Elizabeth Ritchie both encouraged and alarmed her because her own religious experience seemed so meager in comparison with the simplicity and heavenly grace of Elizabeth's conversation and manners. Frances continued to profit from the spiritual guidance of Sarah Crosby and Ann Tripp and from attending the preaching of Wesley and other Methodists, and even from meeting with a select band despite not having joined the society. Interestingly, despite the impact of these encounters and the frequent exchange of letters with Sarah Crosby, Ann Tripp, and Elizabeth Ritchie, she did not formally join the Methodists until December 1780—at last obtaining her mother's consent—after seven years of attending the society meetings as a visitor.[106]

An Unhappy First Marriage

Upon her mother's death only a few months later, Frances found comfort in prayer, and she found solace and a longing to be wholly given up to God as she read Mary Bosanquet's tract *Jesus, Altogether Lovely.*[107] To her surprise, one of Lady Huntingdon's Calvinist preachers, the Reverend Mr. Wren, proposed marriage to her. She was not inclined to accept at first, particularly as there were significant theological differences between them, and her journal shows no indication of romantic attachment or even particular affection. However, on September 14, 1782, they were married, but because of her husband's resentment against anyone connected with the Wesleyan Methodists, it was an unhappy marriage.[108] Mr. Wren died August 4, 1784, and her brother Charles died about three weeks after that, and Frances quickly returned to the nurturing environment of the bands and classes and the love feasts at which she experienced such significant spiritual mentoring and guidance.[109]

Partners in Marriage and Ministry: Frances and John Pawson

Frances was not single again for long, but this prospective bridegroom was a Methodist preacher named John Pawson. Upon learning that Frances was widowed, he wrote to Alexander Mather, another Methodist preacher, asking if Mrs. Mather would find out if Frances would be amenable to a proposal of marriage from him. Apparently receiving encouragement, Pawson came from Manchester to York to visit Frances, telling her frankly that since his wife and her husband had been taken away by Providence, he thought they might be happy together. Like her first proposal, this one lacked romance or passion, and in her journal entry she wryly notes,

> He felt himself capable of a rational affection for me in the Lord; though he could never speak of that love, of which many made their boast. . . . After he was gone, though I was a little surprised at the coolness of his address, yet I felt a calm, and confidence in the Lord, and a hallowed serenity on my soul. I felt none of that perturbation, hesitation, and uncertainty, which had followed me, at every step, in my first marriage. The spirit of prayer and intercession rested upon me most of the day.[110]

However, Frances had a calm sense of the rightness of the union, and they were married on August 14 in York, moving just a few days later to Edinburgh. They found happiness together, for they were united in their convictions and were loyal, supportive partners in ministry. Her example was critical in enabling John Pawson to write and preach confidently about sanctification as a possibility for all believers, and in a letter to Charles Atmore, he praises Frances as a wonderful advocate for Christian perfection because she had experienced its sweetness herself.[111] In Edinburgh, she became involved in the leadership of a class, spending much of her time counseling the members, and she formed a band along with Lady Darcy Maxwell, one of the most prominent Scottish supporters of Methodism. Journal entries grew rarer, as she found less time to write due to her busy schedule.[112]

When they were stationed in Leeds, Frances found "many kindred spirits," like the spiritually mature Dorothy Downes, who was both the wife and sister of Methodist preachers herself. While in Leeds, Frances was delighted to renew her friendship with Elizabeth

Ritchie, who visited her for several days in 1788.[113] These intimate spiritual friendships with like-minded Methodist women were vital for Frances's spiritual growth, and she admired the way Dorothy Downes advised a woman who was seeking full salvation. "She thought the first concern of many should be to get restored to a justified state, and then to seek the perfect love of God."[114] She was likewise impressed by Elizabeth Ritchie, finding her conversation to be "full of life and seasoned with salt."[115] At one class meeting, Frances was greatly edified by Elizabeth's leadership style and her method of spiritual direction. She gave advice to each woman present, depending on her need, counseling Frances herself to "be still and to know God."

When Conference appointed John Pawson to Leeds a second time in 1799, Frances, Sarah Crosby, Ann Tripp, and a Miss Rhodes spent much time in religious conversation together, and her journal abounds with praise of them.[116] The importance of these "Mothers in Israel" in the development and maintenance of Frances Pawson's faith cannot be overemphasized. Often she painstakingly copied into her journal passages from their letters, notes taken from sermons and exhortations of other women, and transcriptions of spiritual experience accounts from the *Arminian Magazine*.[117] As her own faith grew and deepened in holiness, a progression in the letters between Frances and Sarah Crosby reveals a change as the former relationship of mentor and learner blossomed into a more mutual sharing of support.[118]

Marriage to John Pawson was also an important source of mutual strength and comfort, and they presented a united front when controversy erupted within Conference in 1795 and again in the early years of the nineteenth century. Alexander Kilham had led a group of preachers to refuse to sign the Plan of Pacification that attempted to settle disputes over administration of the sacrament, separation from the Church of England, and the authority of Conference.[119] John Pawson was among the leaders of Conference particularly resented by Kilham. Frances had wrestled in prayer with God, hoping for a spirit of forbearance and acknowledgment of wrongs done; but it was not to be, and Kilham led five thousand Methodists to form the New Connexion in 1797.[120]

There were other difficulties and griefs to bear as well. Her dear friend Sarah Crosby died in late 1804, prompting Frances to write, "She has been to me a friend, dear as my own soul, and that from my first setting out in religion. Her memory will be dear to me forever. Though dead, she seems still talking to me, and number of her sayings crowd on my remembrance."[121]

Frances herself was quite ill in 1805, and no sooner did she begin to improve than her husband of twenty-one years died on March 19, 1806, leaving her a widow for the second time. She grieved for him, recollecting that his "affection for me was great, and the provision he has made for me is ample. But, ah, he is gone."[122] A letter from Ann Tripp shows the way the connection of women compassionately leaped into action, as several of them made attempts to find a place for Frances to settle in widowhood. Ann offers her comfort, saying,

> You are now peculiarly called to the exercise of patient resignation to the will of God, and faith in him as a God of providence, whose tender care I believe you will more than ever prove. May he who has promised to be with you night and day so divinely support you that you may upon the mournful occasion be raised above those painful feelings and depressions, your weakness of body, etc., may expose you to. Yet a little while and I trust we shall join our dear friend in the realms of light and glory. They are still near in spirit, how near, who can tell.[123]

As her strength failed and death approached, Frances's faith remained strong and her mind undimmed. A regular visitor, Mr. Thomas Stanley, gave an account of her last day, during which her class met at her house, in her bedchamber at her insistence. She told them, "I have been above thirty years a Methodist, and I shall die one." She died a few hours later, faith unshaken, a Methodist to the end.[124]

FIVE

Mary Fletcher's Legacy

Mentoring Other Women

Mary Fletcher's penetrating insights into the tender yet fierce and protective maternal love of God in Christ and her intense sense of call found expression in her own mentoring and mothering of other Methodist women throughout her life, especially as she grew older. She was a source of inspiration and guidance for women across the Methodist connexion. But many men also greatly valued her ministry, having experienced their conversions under her preaching, and preachers who were stationed in Madeley reverently cited her example in their sermons and conversations for years after her death.[1]

In her remaining years, Mary continued to write in her diary, keeping a somewhat sporadic account of her spiritual health, her sermons, her class and band meetings, and her meditations on various aspects of discipleship. The experience of sanctification was of great importance to Methodists, and a keen desire to receive more and more of the grace of holiness pervaded her thought. In her entry dated April 4, 1793, she muses about the different ways people expressed their own experiences of Christian perfection. One person might feel a degree of faith that continually unites her or him to God through the blood of Christ, while another person might describe it as abiding in Christ and feeling nothing contrary to love. Mary speaks of her own growth in grace and sanctification, and she rejoices, "Being taken into Christ, as a drop of water into the ocean, I lose myself in him, and find in him my all, for time and for eternity. Now a measure of this state I do feel; and I feel strong drawings to expect a clearer fellowship,—a throwing open the everlasting doors of my soul, and a more powerful entrance of the King of glory."[2]

In addition to her guidance of the women of her household, particularly Sally Lawrence and Mary Tooth, Mary frequently corresponded with many Methodist women who asked for her advice on all manner of spiritual issues, particularly this topic of Christian perfection. An exchange of letters from 1792 and 1793 between her and a Mrs. Dalby in Leicestershire was published in the *Methodist Magazine* in 1818 as a model of how to go about seeking holiness of life and heart. In the first one, dated December 26, 1792, Mary responds to Mrs. Dalby's desire for counsel regarding her pursuit of sanctification by pointing to her own experience and suggesting a passage of scripture as a guide for her prayer and reflection, though she referred to many more biblical texts throughout the letter.[3]

In Mrs. Dalby's letter to Mary Fletcher, she had apparently asked about the quickest or shortest way to holiness. In good Wesleyan Methodist fashion, Mary speaks out of the knowledge gained over years of faithful discipleship, and she describes holiness as a free gift of God that one may certainly expect to receive at any moment, not by waiting inactively or in stillness but rather in expectant prayer.

> As to the manner of seeking, I have always found private prayer the truest touchstone. I do not mean it was never well with me when prayer was difficult. No, that is not the mark. But when I labor most in prayer, I get best forward. When I am very conversant with the throne of grace, I soon discern there is a passage form that to the holy of holies, and a continual look brings a continual power. For while we abide in Jesus, he stands as walls and bulwarks of salvation round the believing soul. In that spot may you and I for ever dwell.[4]

Feeling led to direct Mrs. Dalby to study and meditate upon the prayer of Jabez in 1 Chronicles 4:10, Mary recommends that she model her own prayers after it and ask that God enlarge her "coast" just as Jabez had requested God to do for him. Mary tells her five ways in which she can look to God to do so. First, Mrs. Dalby should pray for God to enlarge her "coast of prayer" so that she may learn to pray without ceasing. Second, Mrs. Dalby should pray that God would enlarge her "coast of understanding" and give her a capacity for spiritual things so that she might be rooted and grounded in love (Ephesians 3:17), and third, that God would enlarge her capacity for the spiritual affections, especially for the perfect love that casts out fear.

Fourth, Mary directs her to ask for an enlargement of coast that would enable her to be an advocate who could lead others in the more excellent way, that is, of love; and then fifth, above all, Mary advises her to seek for her "coast of faith" to be enlarged, calling faith "the uniting principle which, as the neck, joins to our sacred head, his body, the church."[5] She closes with mention of her bodily weakness and pain, saying that her poor lame hand and head have for once obeyed her heart's commands by allowing her to write this letter, and she blesses Mrs. Dalby with the promise of prayers for the rich love of Jesus to be made known to her and to her loved ones.

Mothering Sally Lawrence: The Staff of Mary's Old Age

The theme of various ailments and illnesses began to crop up more frequently in her writings, yet Mary Fletcher continued finding in them new opportunities to praise God. In 1793 she suffered from a tumor in her breast, which over time simply disappeared, an occurrence she attributed to the work of God; and in 1794 she complained of being "poorly in body" and experiencing great fatigue, dizziness, and confusion accompanied by fever and pain. "Yet when the hour of meeting, whether of people or children comes, I am enabled to get through the duty, and sometimes with uncommon power. . . . My Lord does all things well."[6]

After John Fletcher's death, Mary had committed herself to preserving and shaping their shared legacy through her preaching and writing and by editing and using his writings as a resource, and this reverent dedication to keeping memory and ministry alive was also lived out through her close mentoring and mothering of Sally Lawrence and Mary Tooth.[7] The relationship between Mary and Sally Lawrence was close and intimate and was in many ways an extension and continuation of the prior intense friendship between Mary Fletcher and Sally's aunt Sarah Ryan.[8] Sally was protégé, servant, daughter, fellow preacher and leader, and a spiritual heir to the tradition of female preachers epitomized in Mary Bosanquet Fletcher and her wider circle. From her earliest childhood days, as part of the Bosanquet and then Fletcher households, Sally had been immersed in an atmosphere of prayer, self-denial, and service.[9]

In adulthood, Sally served Mary as her housekeeper and manager of daily affairs in the household, but Mary's affection for her far exceeded that of a mistress for a favored servant. Mary truly had mentored her, nurtured her, and mothered Sally for most of Sally's life. Their relationship grew more egalitarian as it progressed, and despite Mary Fletcher's years of spiritual experience, age, and economic standing, she felt Sally the superior in spirituality, noting that even though she had reared Sally, she (Mary) wished to learn from *her*:

> I have not such a degree of the Spirit as she has. But I will bless thee, O Lord, that I am permitted to make her way; and will with pleasure do more of the little things of the house, that she may have more leisure to carry thy truth about among souls. She is a faithful follower of the Lamb, and though she has been my orphan to bring up, I now desire to tread in her steps.[10]

Sally's upbringing in a community of strong, pious women accustomed to serving and caring for their neighbors, to preaching the gospel and leading others to growth in holiness, and to devoting themselves wholeheartedly to Christ left a profound imprint on her life. Mary came to look upon her as her successor, viewing her as an inheritor of her aunt Sarah Ryan's spirit as well as the heir of a measure of John Fletcher's spirit and mission.[11] Pointing to the biblical examples of the female prophets Deborah, Priscilla, Anna, and Huldah, as well as to Peter's sermon in Acts on the prophesy of Joel 2, Mary nurtured Sally in the belief that she, too, was one of the daughters who was called and moved by the Spirit to prophesy.[12] Sally was confirmed at the parish church in Leeds as a teenager and joined the Methodist society, and Mary continually encouraged her growth in faith, nurturing the many gifts she saw in Sally.

Among Sally's gifts were a deep compassion for the sick and a strong maternal love for children. Indeed, Mary described Sally as an obedient, eternal child herself.[13] A local man once visited, telling Mary that his daughter was ill with an infectious fever and that she longed to see Sally. As Mary and Sally talked it over, Mary naturally worried about the possibility of Sally becoming ill, though Sally was perfectly prepared to call upon the young woman. Describing Sally as her "greatest consolation, next to God, and useful as a right hand," Mary wrestled with the decision, especially as she remembered that her beloved husband John had died of a fever, but she concluded that she could not refuse Sally's devoting her life to God's glory. Echoing the obedience of Abraham, she cried out, "No, my Lord, my Saviour, no. I offer up every Isaac to thy will."[14] Sally went and ministered to the woman's spiritual needs and did not herself become infected, though her strength and stamina were never great.

Sally often went door to door in Madeley, visiting the poor and downtrodden, holding meetings across the parish despite knowing how ridiculous she appeared in the eyes of some of the people she encountered. However, "such an intense love did she feel toward them at the very time they were ridiculing her that she has told me it seemed she could with pleasure submit to be bound to a stake and burned, if it might but draw these souls to choose the way of life."[15] Boldly, she even took her ministry into pubs, and there were some who experienced salvation on account of her ministry there. Sally's method of leading worship and publicly speaking was strikingly similar to that of Susanna Wesley in the Epworth rectory, decades before:

After singing and prayer, to read some life, experience, or some awakened author, stopping now and then, to explain and apply it as the Lord gave her utterance. And several, who are now lively believers in our connexion, were brought in through that means. But in every step she inquired of the Lord, fearing much to take one out of his order.[16]

In addition, for four years she preached every other Sunday evening in a nearby village, feeling powerfully called to continue serving among the miners and their families as it seemed the fulfillment of a dream she once had of sowing corn. Mary recorded that Sally's word was received by many there, and they lamented when she could no longer meet with them, praying for the restoration of her health. Unfortunately, she was not robust and was weak for many years, probably suffering from tuberculosis, but she kept pushing through her pain and frailty to speak to sinners, pleading for their repentance.

Her mother in Christ, Mary, said that the zeal of the Lord truly did eat her up, and Mary was inspired by Sally's patience even in her illness: "My dear child, what does she suffer. Yet how patient and passive in the hand of God. I seem left to suffer; yet I am wonderfully supported too."[17] In her anticipatory grief over Sally's impending death, Mary pours out her heart in her journal, reflecting that

she has been as the tenderest of daughters to me; a spiritual friend both to soul and body. A most useful housekeeper, and the best of nurses. In short, the staff of my old age. . . . In the work of God she is also admirably useful, and together we get through a good deal. . . . But I will encourage myself in the Lord. We shall not be parted. She goes a little before, and I shall follow after.[18]

Mary's private thoughts in her diary reveal the ups and downs of her emotions as she witnessed the steady decline in Sally's health, and perhaps not surprisingly, she discovers that worship at church is a source of both comfort and sorrow.

As I sat in my pew at church, I thought, I must now go to the table alone. Once I had my dear husband there, and my child at my side. Now, as Naomi, I must say, *I went out full, but return empty.* As I knelt at the table, it seemed as if her spirit was one with mine. . . . I said, Lord, look upon us.

As she listened for God to speak to her heart, she seemed to hear a reassurance that they were in the care of the Most High, and she humbly recounts that this "so melted my heart, I could not help bursting into tears. But they were tears of gratitude."[19]

That same acceptance and resignation to what they termed the will of God pervaded Sally's life; and even on her deathbed, when she could not swallow nor speak without pain, she praised God for the "sweet communion" she had with Jesus, and she repeated verses from hymns as she continued to give thanks to God. As she lay dying, she reported seeing paradise and heaven opened before her, claiming that the blood of Jesus had cleansed her from all sin. When she could no longer speak, she lifted her head to indicate to Mary Fletcher that she was still sensing the ministering presence of angels, "and at seven o'clock, Wednesday, December 3, 1800, without a further struggle, her happy spirit took its flight to feast with Jesus' priests and kings."[20]

Mary's account of Sally's "devoted life and happy death" was read to the society, and she tried to rely upon her faith as she mourned the loss of her beloved daughter and companion, though her grief was intense as she endured this fresh sorrow:

> But O, what a loss do I sustain. God only knows what she was to me, and Himself alone can fill the aching void: What adds to the weight is, I have not that communion with God I long for. I am amazed at the resignation which I feel. Yes, I do, I will adore him, for taking away my all from me. I fear I hung too much on her . . . I begin this year as an hermit: ah. That I may end it as a saint. Come, Lord Jesus, and fulfill all thy gracious promises to my waiting soul.[21]

Thus it was that Mary's designated successor, her dear child and companion, died fifteen years before Mary herself.[22] In her account of Sally's suffering and death, the tradition of retaining and retelling the stories of the lives and ministries of women continued. Just as Mary had faithfully recorded an account of Sarah Ryan, her spiritual mother, so too she preserved the story of her spiritual daughter and Sarah's niece, Sally. This act of love was an ongoing testament to the shared life of Methodist women and "the interconnections between relationship and authorship, self-representation and biography, within a spiritual tradition and manuscript circle that spans the generations."[23]

Mary was comforted by a vision shortly after Sally's death in which she beheld a community of believers in heaven, particularly Sally herself and Mary's beloved husband John Fletcher, both dressed in dazzling white. In her vision, Mary's "little girl" repeatedly called out, "My mummy is coming," which caused Mary to exclaim that the Lord has many ways to comfort his children and to remind us that the family above and the family below are one.[24] Fortunately, she was not left all alone, for the other longtime member of the household, Mary Tooth, was still with her, and Mary Fletcher's "pleasing and instructive" discourses and sermons insured that her preaching meetings still drew large congregations from near and far.[25] Mary Fletcher was still a source of encouragement and a pattern of holy boldness to other women preachers just as she had been for many years, though her spiritual direction was expressed more through the medium of letters than of face-to-face visits due to her infirmity.

Mentoring: Encouraging Mary Barritt Taft and Elizabeth Collett

In October or November 1803, Mary Barritt Taft wrote to Mary Fletcher, the first known exchange of letters between these two most prominent women preachers of the early Methodist revival. Mary Taft was one of the most successful evangelists among those early women preachers, and her style sometimes provoked opposition that was overcome less by argument and more by witnessing the consistent fruit of her preaching.[26]

In the letter, Mary Taft respectfully notes that she had long wanted to make Mary Fletcher's acquaintance but had felt unworthy, but she now embarks on this correspondence because of her distress over the swirling controversy over women preachers. After hearing Mary Fletcher's moving account of Sally Lawrence's labors for the Lord and her pious death, her heart was greatly troubled and grieved that the account published in the *Methodist Magazine* omitted any mention of Sally Lawrence "speaking for God or of her sowing the seed of eternal life." She is emboldened to ask if Mary Fletcher had deliberately left that out or if it was the work of the editor, Joseph Benson. Modestly, Mary Taft then mentions her own intensive labors, inquires if Mary is still laboring for the Lord herself, and requests a letter from Mary at her earliest convenience.[27]

On November 28, 1803, Mary Fletcher penned a response that includes a brief account of her own call and experience as a preacher and leader of Christian communities as well as a commendation of Mary Taft's labors "for the cause of our adorable Jesus"[28] and encouragement for her continued preaching and leading. Referring briefly to her shortness of breath and other continual health problems, she explains that she herself cannot travel as much as before but that she continues to minister in her preaching room and to lead six or seven meetings a week.

Continuing to style the call of women to preach an "extraordinary" one, she emphasizes to Mary Taft that the leading of the Lord may change and be quite different during different times of one's life. Her own style of proclamation had in fact undergone a change, as she often expounded on part or all of a chapter of the Bible. Sally Lawrence had generally tended to read from a pious author, stopping to explain as she went; but, Mary Fletcher says, each woman must follow her own order, trusting in God to guide her in the right way.[29]

Another woman who sought Mary's insight and advice was Elizabeth Collett, one of the best-known female preachers in Cornwall. Greatly influenced by the example and mentoring of Ann Gilbert, the first Cornish woman to preach, Elizabeth enjoyed the guidance and support of superintending minister Joseph Taylor when she began preaching in 1782. She was known for her power in public prayer and preaching, and she founded no less than three societies.[30] Like Ann Gilbert and Sarah Crosby and Susanna Wesley before her, Elizabeth began speaking publicly to fill a perceived need. She was urged to exhort at a society meeting when the itinerant preacher failed to show up, and because she felt the Spirit constraining her to respond, she did so. This positive experience was confirmed by the fruit of the Spirit among the people in attendance, and she continued exhorting, usually without a text, across Cornwall.[31]

Married with eleven children, she retired from an active preaching ministry in 1804, probably because of declining health, and preached her final sermon in a chapel built by her husband. She wrote to Mary Fletcher for comfort and counsel a few years after retirement in a time of distress and trouble, and Mary's response was to reassure her in the midst of the physical suffering that was creating even greater spiritual turmoil in Elizabeth's heart.[32]

Because Elizabeth was so ill, she did not feel the same joy in the Lord she had once experienced, and Mary consoled her by saying, "It is true your bodily sufferings may keep you sometimes from feeling that degree of joy which some may feel who have less faith and love. . . . Do not measure your state of grace by your degree of joy, but by power to hang on the word of the Lord." As a way of encouraging Elizabeth to endure with patience her own weakness and pain and to trust in God's goodness, Mary then related a story of the recent "good death" of a man in her community and the way his years of pain had drawn him closer to God. She closed by blessing Elizabeth: "May the Lord put his arms of love underneath you."[33]

The Death of Mary Bosanquet Fletcher: Mary Tooth Preserves Her Legacy

For several years, Mary Fletcher, Sally Lawrence, and Mary Tooth had formed a sort of threefold ministry along with the curate of the parish church and the itinerant Wesleyan preachers.[34] After the death of Sally Lawrence, Mary Tooth filled the void left by her absence, becoming the "right hand" of Mary Fletcher. Like Sally, she originally held a position as a servant in the household but swiftly became a protégé and beloved companion and eventually Mary's designated successor to the leadership of the Methodist societies in Madeley.[35] In this capacity, Mary Tooth remained in the Madeley community until her own death in 1843.[36]

Zechariah Taft opens his biographical sketch of Mary Tooth by describing her as "the constant companion and assistant of that mother in Israel, the late Mrs. Fletcher."[37] One of nine children in a Birmingham family, Mary Tooth first became acquainted with Mary Fletcher and Sally Lawrence when she was working at a school in Madeley in 1795, and she came to live in the Fletcher household just prior to Sally Lawrence's death.

The intense relationship between Mary Fletcher and Mary Tooth was reminiscent of the closeness of Mary Fletcher and Sarah Ryan, and under Mary Fletcher's tutelage Mary Tooth became increasingly active in the parish as a preacher in the tithe barn and elsewhere in Shropshire and as a class leader.[38] She was regarded by Mary Fletcher as a gift of God without whom she could not manage her life and ministerial obligations. Her critical role in helping maintain some control over the publication and distribution of Mary Fletcher's writings after her death underlines the importance of female net-works of collaboration in the preservation and transmission of their diaries and sermons, as well as their autobiographies and accounts of each other's lives; and just as Mary Fletcher had recorded the death of Sally Lawrence, so Mary Tooth faithfully transcribed an account of Mary Fletcher's death in 1815.[39]

Mary Tooth's sister Rosamond came to live in Madeley as part of the Fletcher household in 1808, and after Mary Fletcher's death, Rosamond played a supportive role to her sister just as Sally Law-rence and Mary Tooth had done for Mary Fletcher, remaining there with her sister until her own death in 1832.[40] In large part, in the years following the death of Mary Fletcher, Mary Tooth carried the banner for women preachers, stepping into the place left by the bold Mothers in Israel who went before them, connecting with dozens of women still preaching despite the 1803 restrictions placed on them by Conference. Like her "mother" Mary Fletcher, Mary Tooth felt a strong call to public ministry and was determined to serve within Methodism. Regarding herself as the successor to Mary Fletcher, Mary Tooth reflected on Mary Fletcher's death:

> I alone was her constant companion without being separated scarcely a day for more than 15 years; I have endeavoured, while my mind has been exercised with the most painful feelings of heart-felt sorrow for the loss of the best of friends; the wisest of Counsellors, and the tenderest of parents, to set down a few circumstances related to the close of a life surpassing in usefulness most of her fellow mortals.
>
> It was upon the 9th [of December] of 1815, a day never to be forgotten by me that my Elijah was taken to heaven. O that the mantle might rest on me.[41]

Mary Bosanquet Fletcher's mantle had indeed fallen on Mary Tooth, who successfully carried on the Madeley ministry and its Anglican-Methodist partnership, sustained important supportive relationships with other preaching women, and transmitted the story of that well-respected "Mother in Israel" so that future generations would be edified and inspired by her example and faithful witness. Writing an obituary of Mary for Joseph Benson, editor of the *Methodist Magazine,* she revealed the depth of affection between Mary Fletcher and herself, a closeness that was stronger even than biological ties:

> To me she was more than a mother. I have felt for her all that a child can feel for a parent; and her death has occasioned me the most painful conflict I have ever endured. I miss her day by day and cannot but deeply mourn the loss of such a counsellor and friend; though, through divine grace, I do not murmur at the dispensation. For twenty years, I had the unspeakable advantage of her friendship, her maternal love, and prayers; for more than the last fifteen of which, I was so highly privileged as to abide under her roof, and be

scarcely separated from her for one day during the whole time. Her affection to me was so great, that she often said, to lose me would be the heaviest earthly affliction that could befall her; but she believed the Lord would never call her to drink that bitter cup. In this, and many other things of a similar nature, our gracious Lord was pleased to give her the desire of her heart.[42]

In typical Methodist fashion, Mary Tooth's account of Mary Fletcher's death reported her peace and joy at the end.

There was at last neither sigh, groan, or struggle, but all the appearance of a person in the most composed slumber . . . I then perceived, the moment she had so much longed for had arrived. For I think I have heard her some hundreds of times exclaim, with the most vehement desire, "O, my Jesus, when shall I fly to thy arms." She was always looking and waiting for the happy moment when she should gain the blissful shore.[43]

The epitaph composed to honor Mary Bosanquet Fletcher bore eloquent witness to the deep love and profound grief of the people of Madeley and the debt they owed her for promoting the unity of Church and Chapel there for so many years. Although it does not mention her preaching and instead frames her work around John Fletcher's ministry, it is a testament to a remarkable woman who was a preacher, a leader, a mentor, a counselor, a pastor, and indeed a true Mother in Israel. It reads:

During the long period in which she survived her husband, she continued to tread the path in which he left her and ministered with ardent zeal and self denying beneficence to the spiritual and temporal wants of his flock. By the influence of her example and instruction dissensions were healed and schism in the Church of Christ prevented and it was her constant and earnest endeavour to induce all around her to dwell in unity and Godly love.[44]

Conclusion

Of all the praise heaped upon certain Methodist women after their deaths, nothing was more affectionate or significant than calling them "Mothers in Israel." All Methodist women were called sister; being a mother was on a completely different level. Mothers in Israel provided a home for itinerant preachers to sleep and a place where they could preach regularly; they routinely held class and band meetings and led worship, even preached, when the traveling preacher was absent; and they died good, holy deaths while praising God and exhorting their loved ones to walk as Christ walked.[45] Their obedience to God pushed the boundaries of accepted behavior for women, challenged the expectations of a woman's place in public life, brought the gospel of Jesus Christ to rowdy people in unconventional places, and paved the way for the eventual ordination of their spiritual daughters. To them, we owe a debt of gratitude we cannot pay—for their holy boldness, their stubborn obedience, their honest self-appraisal, and their wise spiritual counsel to the people called Methodists. It is my hope and prayer that this book will in some small way be a down payment on that debt and serve as a "remembrancer" (in Mary Bosanquet Fletcher's words) of our need to imitate Christ as fearlessly and faithfully as did those Mothers in Israel.

Endnotes

Introduction

1. Richard Heitzenrater, preface to first edition, *Wesley and the People Called Methodists* (Nashville: Abingdon Press, 2013), xi.

2. Henry D. Rack, introduction to first edition, *Reasonable Enthusiast* (Nashville: Abingdon Press, 1992), ix–x.

3. Heitzenrater, *Wesley and the People Called Methodists*, 109, 126–127, 264–265.

4. Vicki Tolar Burton, *Spiritual Literacy in John Wesley's Methodism* (Waco, TX: Baylor University Press, 2008), 102.

5. Tolar Burton, *Spiritual Literacy*, 175.

6. Deborah M. Valenze, *Prophetic Sons and Daughters: Female Preaching and Popular Religion in Industrial England* (Princeton, N.J.: Princeton University Press, 1985), 35–36.

7. Tolar Burton, *Spiritual Literacy*, 159.

8. Anna M. Lawrence, *One Family Under God* (Philadelphia: University of Pennsylvania Press, 2011), 85–86.

Chapter One

1. Adam Clarke, *Memoirs of the Wesley Family* (London: J. And T. Clarke, 1823), 361.

2. Rack, *Reasonable Enthusiast*, 50.

3. Samuel Rogal, *Susanna Annesley Wesley: A Biography of Strength and Love* (Bristol, IN: Wyndham Hill Press, 2001), 175.

4. John Newton, "Wesley and Women," in *John Wesley: Contemporary Perspectives*, ed. John Stacey (London: Epworth Press, 1988), 131–134.

5. W. Reginald Ward and Richard P. Heitzenrater, eds., *The Bicentennial Edition of the Works of John Wesley: Vol. 19, Journals and Diaries II (1738–1743)*, entry for July 30, 1742 (Nashville: Abingdon Press, 1993), 284.

6. Rogal, *Susanna Annesley Wesley*, 141.

7. John Newton, *Susanna Wesley and the Puritan Tradition* (London: Epworth Press, 2002), 207.

8. Newton, *Susanna Wesley and the Puritan Tradition*, 17.

9. Charles Wallace, ed., introduction to *Susanna Wesley: The Complete Writings* (New York: Oxford University Press, 1997), 19.

10. Tolar Burton, *Spiritual Literacy*, 2.

11. Charles Wallace, "'Some Stated Employment of Your Mind': Reading, Writing, and Religion in the Life of Susanna Wesley," *Church History* 47, no. 3 (1989): 355–356.

12. Rogal, *Susanna Annesley Wesley*, 175.

13. Wallace, ed., *Susanna Wesley: Complete Writings*, 18.

14. Newton, *Susanna Wesley and the Puritan Tradition*, 19.

15. Mary Greetham, *Susanna Wesley: Mother of Methodism* (Peterborough: Foundery Press, 1988), 4.

16. Frank Baker, "Salute to Susanna," *Methodist History*, 3–12 (April 1969): 4.

17. Frank Baker, "Susanna Wesley: Puritan, Parent, Pastor, Protagonist, Pattern," in *Women in New Worlds*, vol. 2, ed. Keller, Queen, and Thomas (Nashville: Abingdon Press, 1982), 113.

18. Rogal, *Susanna Annesley Wesley*, 13.

19. Wallace, ed., *Susanna Wesley: Complete Writings*, 71.

20. Wallace, ed., *Susanna Wesley: Complete Writings*, 71; Greetham, *Susanna Wesley: Mother of Methodism*, 10.

21. Newton, *Susanna Wesley and the Puritan Tradition*, 65.

22. Arnold Dallimore, *Susanna Wesley: The Mother of John & Charles Wesley* (Grand Rapids: Baker Book House, 1993), 23–24.

23. Baker, "Susanna Wesley: Puritan, Parent, Pastor, Protagonist, Pattern," 114.

24. Dallimore, *Susanna Wesley*, 32.

25. Rogal, *Susanna Annesley Wesley*, 20.

26. Newton, *Susanna Wesley and Puritan Tradition*, 69.

27. Wallace, ed., *Complete Writings*, 35.

28. Clarke, *Memoirs*, 94.

29. Clarke, *Memoirs*, 95.

30. Robert Walmsley, "John Wesley's Parents: Quarrel and Reconciliation," *Proceedings of the Wesley Historical Society*, 29, no. 3 (1953): 50–51.

31. Walmsley, "John Wesley's Parents," 50–51.

32. Wallace, ed., *Complete Writings*, 35.

33. Dallimore, *Susanna Wesley*, 49–50.

34. Wallace, ed., *Complete Writings*, 37.

35. Wallace, ed., *Complete Writings*, 37–38.

36. Dallimore, *Susanna Wesley*, 51.

37. Walmsley, "John Wesley's Parents," 55.

38. Dallimore, *Susanna Wesley*, 51–52.

39. Patricia Crawford, *Women and Religion in England 1500–1720* (New York: Routledge Press, 1996), 96.

40. Wallace, ed., *Complete Writings*, 39.

41. Dallimore, *Susanna Wesley*, 53.

42. Walmsley, "John Wesley's Parents," 57.

43. Greetham, *Susanna Wesley: Mother of Methodism*, 7.

44. Newton, *Susanna Wesley and the Puritan Tradition*, 73.

45. Rogal, *Susanna Annesley Wesley*, 36.

46. Rachel Rigdon and Thomas Webster, "His Mother's Child: On Susanna Wesley's Great Influence upon Her Son, John Wesley," *Perkins Student Journal* (2014–2015): 31–32.

47. Tolar Burton, *Spiritual Literacy*, 41.

48. Claire Wolfteich, "A Difficult Love: Mother as Spiritual Guide in the Writing of Susanna Wesley," *Methodist History*, 38, no. 1 (October 1999): 53–54.

49. Rigdon and Webster, "His Mother's Child," 31–32.

50. Wallace, ed., *Complete Writings*, 367.

51. Baker, "Salute to Susanna," 6.

52. Wallace, ed., *Complete Writings*, 71.

53. David Butler, "Look for the Mother to Find the Son," *Epworth Review*, 25, no. 4 (October 1998): 90.

54. Tolar Burton, *Spiritual Literacy*, 39–40.

55. Butler, "Look for the Mother to Find the Son," 91.

56. Tolar Burton, *Spiritual Literacy*, 41–42.

57. Baker, "Susanna Wesley: Puritan, Parent, Pastor, Protagonist, Pattern," 118.

58. Wallace, ed., *Complete Writings*, 373.

59. Baker, "Susanna Wesley: Puritan, Parent, Pastor, Protagonist, Pattern," 122.

60. A. T. Quiller–Couch, *Hetty Wesley* (New York, London: Macmillan Co., 1903), 283–286. https: archive.org. details. cu31924013537901. Accessed December 4, 2019.

61. Rogal, *Susanna Annesley Wesley*, 99.

62. Frank Baker, ed., *The Bicentennial Edition of the Works of John Wesley*: Vol. 25, Letters I (1721–1739) letter to Samuel Wesley, Jr (Oxford: Oxford University Press, 1980), 205.

63. Dallimore, *Susanna Wesley: Mother of John and Charles Wesley*, 136.

64. Paul Wesley Chilcote, ed., *Her Own Story: Autobiographical Portraits of Early Methodist Women* (Nashville: Kingswood Books, 2001), 30–31.

65. Wallace, ed., *Complete Writings*, 236.

66. Wallace, ed., *Complete Writings*, 236.

67. Tolar Burton, *Spiritual Literacy*, 42.

68. Wallace, ed., *Complete Writings*, 369–371.

69. Wallace, ed., *Complete Writings*, 372.

70. Rebecca Lamar Harmon, *Susanna: Mother of the Wesleys* (Nashville: Abingdon Press, 1968), 56.

71. Wallace, ed., *Complete Writings*, 237.

72. Newton, *Susanna Wesley and the Puritan Tradition*, 114.

73. Tolar Burton, *Spiritual Literacy*, 61–62.

74. Baker, *Susanna Wesley: Puritan, Parent, Pastor, Protagonist, Pattern*, 120.

75. Wallace, ed., *Complete Writings*, 59–60.

76. Wallace, ed., *Complete Writings*, 59–61.

77. Wallace, ed. *Complete Writings*, 61–62.

78. Wallace, ed., *Complete Writings*, 377.

79. Wallace, ed., *Complete Writings*, 379–380.

80. Wallace, ed., *Complete Writings*, 396.

81. Wallace, ed., *Complete Writings*, 396–397.

82. Wallace, ed., *Complete Writings*, 72.

83. Wallace, ed., *Complete Writings*, 33.

84. Charles Wallace, "Susanna Wesley's Spirituality," *Methodist History* 22, no. 3 (April 1984): 159–160.

85. Butler, "Look for the Mother to Find the Son," 91.

86. Rigdon and Webster, "His Mother's Child," 35.

87. Wallace, ed., *Complete Writings*, 235.

88. Wallace, ed., *Complete Writings*, 80.

89. Tolar Burton, *Spiritual Literacy*, 62.

90. Wallace, ed., *Complete Writings*, 109.

91. Albert Outler and Richard P. Heitzenrater, eds., *John Wesley's Sermons: An Anthology* (Nashville: Abingdon Press, 1991), 58.

92. Frank Baker, ed., *The Bicentennial Edition of the Works of John Wesley*. Vol. 25, Letters I (1721–1739) letter to Susanna Wesley February 28,1731. 2 (Nashville: Abingdon Press, 1993), 327–330.

93. Wallace, ed., *Complete Writings*, 176.

94. Charles Wallace, "Susanna Wesley's Spirituality: The Freedom of a Christian Woman," *Methodist History*, 22, no. 3 (April 1984): 161.

95. Wallace, ed., *Complete Writings*, 255.

96. Wallace, ed., *Complete Writings*, 197.

97. Tolar Burton, *Spiritual Literacy*, 45–46.

98. Wallace, ed., *Complete Writings*, 277.

99. Wallace, ed., *Complete Writings*, 277–278.

100. Wallace, ed., *Complete Writings*, 290.

101. Wallace, ed., *Complete Writings*, 208.

102. Wallace, ed., *Complete Writings*, 208–209.
103. Wallace, ed., *Complete Writings*, 222.
104. Wallace, ed., *Complete Writings*, 255.
105. Christine L. Krueger, *The Reader's Repentance*, (Chicago: University of Chicago Press, 1992), 33.
106. Wallace, ed., *Complete Writings*, 176.
107. Wallace, "Susanna Wesley's Spirituality," 161.
108. Krueger, *The Reader's Repentance*, 32.
109. Wolfteich, "A Difficult Love," 56.
110. Baker, "Susanna Wesley," *Women in New Worlds*, 123.
111. Baker, "Susanna Wesley," *Women in New Worlds*, 123.
112. Wallace, ed., *Complete Writings*, 83, 78.
113. Rigdon and Webster, "His Mother's Child," 35.
114. Wallace, ed., *Complete Writings*, 78.
115. Wallace, ed., *Complete Writings*, 79.
116. Wallace, ed., *Complete Writings*, 79.
117. Wallace, ed., *Complete Writings*, 79.
118. Wallace, ed., *Complete Writings*, 81.
119. Tolar Burton, *Spiritual Literacy*, 47.
120. Wallace, ed., *Complete Writings*, 82–83.
121. Tolar Burton, *Spiritual Literacy*, 47.
122. Rigdon and Webster, "His Mother's Child," 35–36.
123. Alan Hayes, "John Wesley and Sophy Hopkey," in *Women in New Worlds*, vol. 2, ed. Keller, Queen, and Thomas (Nashville: Abingdon Press, 1982), 37.
124. Baker, "Susanna Wesley: Puritan, Parent, Pastor, Protagonist, Pattern," 131.
125. Newton, *Susanna Wesley and the Puritan Tradition*, 182.
126. Frank Baker, "Susanna Wesley, Apologist for Methodism," *Proceedings of the Wesley Historical Society*, 35, no. 3 (September 1965): 68–71.
127. Wallace, ed., *Complete Writings*, 464.
128. Wallace, ed., *Complete Writings*, 467.
129. Wallace, ed., *Complete Writings*, 478.
130. Baker, "Susanna Wesley, Apologist for Methodism," 71.
131. Wallace, ed, *Complete Writings*, 190.
132. Wallace, ed., *Complete Writings*, 190.
133. Clarke, *Memoirs*, 336.

Chapter Two

1. Susie C. Stanley, *Holy Boldness: Women Preachers' Autobiographies and the Sanctified Self* (Knoxville: University of Tennessee Press, 2002), 49.
2. Krueger, *The Reader's Repentance*, 32.

3. Tolar Burton, *Spiritual Literacy*, 32.

4. Paul Chilcote, *John Wesley and the Women Preachers of Early Methodism* (Lanham, MD: Scarecrow Press, 1991), 22.

5. Lawrence, *One Family Under God*, 28–29.

6. Baker, ed., *The Works of John Wesley: Bicentennial Edition*, Vol. 25, Letters I (1721–1739) letter to John Hutton and Mr. Fox, November 24, 1738 (Nashville: Abingdon Press, 1993), 488.

7. Patricia Crawford, *Women and Religion in England 1500–1720*, (London: Routledge press, 1996), 97, 93.

8. Jennifer Lloyd, *Women and the Shaping of British Methodism: Persistent Preachers, 1807–1907* (Manchester: Manchester University Press, 2010), 22.

9. Andrew O. Winckles, "'Excuse what deficiencies you will find': Methodist Women and Public Space in John Wesley's *Arminian Magazine*," *Eighteenth Century Studies* 46, no. 3 (2013): 417.

10. Tolar Burton, *Spiritual Literacy*, 152.

11. Tolar Burton, *Spiritual Literacy*, xv.

12. Phyllis Mack, *Heart Religion in the British Enlightenment* (Cambridge: Cambridge University Press, 2008), 137–139.

13. Baker, ed. *Works of John Wesley*, Vol. 25, 87–88.

14. Tolar Burton, *Spiritual Literacy*, xv–xvi.

15. John Telford, ed., *The Letters of the Rev. John Wesley, A.M.* (London: Epworth Press, 1931) http: wesley.nnu.edu. john–wesley. the–letters–of–john–wesley. wesleys–letters–1774, accessed February 15, 2020.

16. Telford, ed., *Letters of John Wesley*.

17. Telford, ed., *Letters of John Wesley*, accessed February 15, 2020. http:wesley.nnu.edu.john–wesley.the–letters–of–john–wesley.wesleys–letters–1776.

18. Mack, *Heart Religion*, 139–143.

19. Mack, *Heart Religion*, 135.

20. Lloyd, *Women and the Shaping of British Methodism*, 21.

21. Paul W. Chilcote, *She Offered Them Christ* (Nashville: Abingdon, 1993), 25.

22. Earl Kent Brown, "Women of the Word," in *Women in New Worlds*, Vol. 1, eds. Keller, Queen, and Thomas, (Nashville: Abingdon Press, 1981), 69.

23. Amy Culley, *British Women's Life Writing, 1760–1840* (New York: Palgrave Publishing, 2014), 25.

24. Thomas M. Morrow, *Early Methodist Women* (London: Epworth Press, 1967), 74.

25. Krueger, *Reader's Repentance*, 42.

26. Stanley, *Holy Boldness*, 56.

27. Culley, *British Women's Life Writing*, 23.

28. Tolar Burton, *Spiritual Literacy*, 152.

29. Chilcote, *Her Own Story*, 14.

30. Krueger, *Reader's Repentance*, 76.

31. Winckles, "'Excuse What Difficiencies You Will Find,'" 419.

32. Tolar Burton, *Spiritual Literacy*, 97.

33. Tolar Burton, *Spiritual Literacy*, 97, 103.

34. "Wesleyan Core Term: Pastor," in *The Wesley Study Bible, NRSV* (Nashville: Abingdon Press, 2009), 1435; Chilcote, *John Wesley and Women Preachers*, 22–23.

35. Rupert E. Davies, ed., *The Works of John Wesley, Bicentennial Edition.*, Vol. 9, *The Methodist Societies: History, Nature, and Design* (Nashville: Abingdon Press, 1989), 69–73.

36. Heitzenrater, *Wesley and the People Called Methodists*, 114–115.

37. Brown, *Women of Mr. Wesley's Methodism*, 11.

38. Lawrence, *One Family Under God*, 38–39.

39. Chilcote, *John Wesley and the Women Preachers of Early Methodism*, 69.

40. Heitzenrater, *Wesley and the People Called Methodists*, 130–131.

41. Telford, ed., *Letters of John Wesley*, October 1776, accessed February 27, 2020 http: wesley.nnu.edu.john–wesley.the–letters–of–john–wesley .wesleys–letters–1776. .

42. Chilcote, *John Wesley and the Women Preachers*, 68, 217.

43. Chilcote, *John Wesley and the Women Preachers*, 87.

44. "Account of Mrs. Sarah Ryan," *Arminian Magazine* II (1779): 300.

45. "Account of Mrs. Sarah Ryan," 309–310.

46. Ted. A. Campbell, ed. *The Works of John Wesley: Bicentennial Edition*, Vol. 27, Letters III (1756–1765), Letter to Sarah Ryan, November 8, 1757. (Nashville: Abingdon Press, 2015), 103–104.

47. Campbell, ed., *Works of John Wesley*, Vol. 27, 112.

48. Mack, *Heart Religion*, 140.

49. Gareth Lloyd, "Sarah Perrin (1721–1787): Early Methodist Exhorter," *Methodist History*, 41, no. 3 (April 2003): 80–81.

50. Lloyd, "Sarah Perrin," 81–82.

51. Chilcote, *John Wesley and the Women Preachers*, 74.

52. Davies, ed., *Works of John Wesley*, Vol. 9, 35–41.

53. Chilcote, *John Wesley and the Women Preachers*, 72.

54. Davies, ed., *Works of John Wesley*, Vol. 9, 274–275.

55. Kenneth J. Collins and Jason E. Vickers, eds., *The Sermons of John Wesley* (Nashville: Abingdon Press, 2013), 349.

56. Phyllis Mack, "Does Gender Matter? Suffering and Salvation in Eighteenth Century Methodism," *Bulletin of the John Rylands University Library of Manchester*, 85, no. 2 and 3 (Summer and Autumn 2003): 163–165.

57. Collins and Vickers, eds., *Sermons of John Wesley*, 349.

58. Collins and Vickers, eds., *Sermons of John Wesley*, 350.

59. Collins and Vickers, eds., *Sermons of John Wesley*, 351.

60. Collins and Vickers, eds., *Sermons of John Wesley*, 354.

61. Brett C. McInelly, "Mothers in Christ" in *Religion, Gender, and Industry: Exploring Church and Methodism in a Local Setting* (Eugene, OR: Pickwick Publications, 2011), 123–125.

62. Gary M. Best, *A Tragedy of Errors*, (Bristol, New Room Publications, 2016), 41, 57.

63. Chilcote, *John Wesley and the Women Preachers*, 73–74.

64. Quoted in Chilcote, *John Wesley and the Women Preachers*, 95.

65. Quoted in Chilcote, *John Wesley and Women Preachers*, 95–96.

66. Earl Kent Brown, *Women of Mr. Wesley's Methodism* (New York: Mellen, 1983), 20.

67. Tolar Burton, *Spiritual Literacy*, 155–156.

68. Brown, *Women in Mr. Wesley's Methodism*, 21.

69. Tolar Burton, *Spiritual Literacy*, 170.

70. W. Reginald Ward and Richard P. Heitzenrater, eds., *The Bicentennial Edition of the Works of John Wesley: Vol. 21, Journals and Diaries IV (1755–1765)*, entry for July 19, 1761 (Nashville: Abingdon Press, 1993), 336.

71. Krueger, *Reader's Repentance*, 52.

72. Tolar Burton, *Spiritual Literacy*, 160.

73. Brown, *Women of Mr. Wesley's Methodism*, 23.

74. Quoted in Burton, *Spiritual Literacy*, 161.

75. Tolar Burton, *Spiritual Literacy*, 24.

76. Chilcote, *Her Own Story*, 18.

77. Ward and Heitzenrater, eds. *The Works of John Wesley, Bicentennial ed., Vol. 20, Journal III 1743–1754*, entry August 13, 1746 (Nashville: Abingdon Press, 1991), 128.

78. Chilcote, *John Wesley and the Women Preachers*, 97.

79. Chilcote, *John Wesley and the Women Preachers*, 196.

80. Chilcote, *Her Own Story*, 218.

81. Chilcote, *Her Own Story*, 218.

82. Tolar Burton, *Her Own Story*, 160.

83. Telford, ed., *Letters of John Wesley*, Accessed February 11, 2020 http:wesley.nnu.edu.john–wesley.the–letters–of–john–wesley.wesleys–letters–1790b.

84. Tolar Burton, *Spiritual Literacy*, 116–117.

85. Telford, ed., *Letters of John Wesley*, Accessed February 9, 2020 http:wesley.nnu.edu.john–wesley.the–letters–of–john–wesley.wesleys–letters–1775.

86. Telford, ed., *Letters of John Wesley*, Accessed February 10, 2020 http:wesley.nnu.edu.john–wesley.the–letters–of–john–wesley.wesleys–letters–1789b.

87. Tolar Burton, *Spiritual Literacy*, 157, 18–19.

88. Krueger, *Reader's Repentance*, 27–28.

89. Chilcote, *John Wesley and the Women Preachers*, 238.

90. Chilcote, *Her Own Story*, 16.

91. Lawrence, *One Family Under God*, 88.

92. Chilcote, *John Wesley and the Women Preachers*, 240.

93. Tolar Burton, *Spiritual Literacy*, 172.

94. David East, "'Lightly Esteemed by Men': The Last Years of Sarah Mallet, One of Mr. Wesley's Female Preachers," *Methodist History*, 42, no. 1 (October 2003): 59.

95. Chilcote, *Her Own Story*, 175.

96. Chilcote, *John Wesley and the Women Preachers*, 232–233.

97. Quoted in Chilcote, *John Wesley and the Women Preachers*, 228.

98. Quoted in East, "'Lightly Esteemed," 62.

99. Leslie F. Church, *More About the Early Methodist People* (London: Epworth Press, 1949), 172.

100. Tolar Burton, *Spiritual Literacy*, 171–172, 176.

101. Chilcote, *Her Own Story*, 15.

102. Culley, *British Women's Life Writing*, 30–32.

103. Culley, *British Women's Life Writing*, 19.

104. Culley, *British Women's Life Writing*, 32.

105. Krueger, *Reader's Repentance*, 76.

106. Mack, *Heart Religion*, 134–135.

Chapter Three

1. Henry Moore, ed., *The Life of Mrs. Mary Fletcher: Consort and Relict of the Rev. John Fletcher, Vicar of Madeley, Salop*, (New York: J. Soule and T. Mason, 1818), 2.

2. Mack, *Heart Religion*, 168.

3. Phyllis Mack and David Wilson, "Mary Fletcher's Bible," in *Dissent and the Bible in Britain 1650–1950*, Scott Mandelbrote and Michael Ledger–Lomas, eds. (Oxford: Oxford University Press, 2013), 58.

4. Culley, *British Women's Life Writing*, 34.

5. Joanna Cruickshank, "'Friend of My Soul:' Constructing Spiritual Friendship in the Autobiography of Mary Fletcher," *Journal for Eighteenth–Century Studies* 32, no. 3 (2009): 374.

6. Culley, *British Women's Life Writing*, 14.

7. David Frudd, "Mary Fletcher as a Source for Spirituality in Methodism," *Angels and Impudent Women: Women in Methodism* (papers given at the 2005 Conference of The Wesley Historical Society), Norma Virgoe, ed., (Loughborough: Teamprint), 84–86.

8. Frudd, "Mary Fletcher as a Source," 100–101.

9. Frudd, "Mary Fletcher as a Source," 101, 85.

10. Culley, *British Women's Life Writing*, 61, 23.

11. Abel Stevens, *Early Methodist Women* (London: Epworth Press, 1967), 66.

12. Frudd, "Mary Fletcher as a Source," 87–88.

13. Culley, *British Women's Life Writing*, 39.

14. Moore, ed., *Life of Mrs. Mary Fletcher*, 22.

15. Moore, ed., *Life of Mrs. Mary Fletcher*, 24.

16. Culley, *British Women's Life Writing*, 39.

17. Moore, ed., *Life of Mrs. Mary Fletcher*, 28.

18. Krueger, *Reader's Repentance*, 33.

19. Krueger, *Reader's Repentance*, 30.

20. Moore, ed., *Life of Mrs. Mary Fletcher*, 33.

21. Moore, ed., *Life of Mrs. Mary Fletcher*, 33–34.

22. Mack, *Heart Religion,* 151.

23. Moore, ed., *Life of Mrs. Mary Fletcher*, 36.

24. D. R. Wilson, "'Thou Shalt Walk with Me in White': Afterlife and Vocation in the Ministry of Mary Bosanquet Fletcher," in *Wesley and Methodist Studies*, 1 (2009): 76–77.

25. Moore, ed., *Life of Mrs. Mary Fletcher*, 38.

26. Moore, ed., *Life of Mrs. Mary Fletcher*, 39–42.

27. Moore, ed., *Life of Mrs. Mary Fletcher*, 34.

28. Culley, *British Women's Life Writing*, 40.

29. Quoted in Mack, *Heart Religion*, 160.

30. Moore, ed., *Life of Mrs. Mary Fletcher*, 43.

31. Moore, ed., *Life of Mrs. Mary Fletcher*, 44.

32. Moore, ed., *Life of Mrs. Mary Fletcher*, 47.

33. Moore, ed., *Life of Mrs. Mary Fletcher*, 46.

34. Moore, ed., *Life of Mrs. Mary Fletcher*, 47.

35. Mack, *Heart Religion*, 151.

36. W. Reginald Ward and Richard P. Heitzenrater, eds., *Works of John Wesley: Vol. 21, Journals and Diaries IV (1755–1765)*, entry for Dec. 1, 1764 (Nashville: Abingdon, 1992), 495.

37. Moore, ed., *Life of Mrs. Mary Fletcher*, 52–53.

38. Mack, *Heart Religion*, 304, 308.

39. Paul W. Chilcote, "Sanctification as Lived by Early Methodist Women," *Methodist History*, 34, no. 2 (January 1996): 101.

40. Joanna Cruickshank, "'Friend of My Soul:' Constructing Spiritual Friendship in the Autobiography of Mary Fletcher," *Journal for Eighteenth–Century Studies* 32, no. 3 (2009), 374.

41. Quoted in Mack, *Heart Religion*, 165.

42. Mack, *Heart Religion*, 147.

43. McInelly, "Mothers in Christ," 125.

44. Culley, *British Women's Life Writing*, 43.

45. Moore, ed., *Life of Mrs. Mary Fletcher*, 54–55.

46. Moore, ed., *Life of Mrs. Mary Fletcher*, 60.

47. Moore, ed., *Life of Mrs. Mary Fletcher*, 65.

48. Mack, *Heart Religion*, 169.

49. W. Reginald Ward and Richard P. Heitzenrater, eds., *The Bicentennial Edition of the Works of John Wesley: Vol. 22, Journals and Diaries V (1765–1775)*, entry for February 12, 1767 (Nashville: Abingdon Press, 1993), 70.

50. Ward and Heitzenrater, eds., *Works of John Wesley, Vol. 22*, entry for November 20, 1767, 110.

51. Moore, ed., *Life of Mrs. Mary Fletcher*, 70–75.

52. Moore, ed., *Life of Mrs. Mary Fletcher*, 83–85.

53. Cruickshank, "'Friend of My Soul,'" 373.

54. Cruickshank, "'Friend of My Soul,'" 378.

55. Moore, ed., *Life of Mrs. Mary Fletcher*, 85.

56. Cruickshank, "'Friend of My Soul,'" 376.

57. Cruickshank, "'Friend of My Soul,'" 382–383.

58. Moore, ed., *Life of Mrs. Mary Fletcher*, 97–98.

59. Moore, ed., *Life of Mrs. Mary Fletcher*, 89–92.

60. Moore, ed., *Life of Mrs. Mary Fletcher*, 94.

61. Moore, ed., *Life of Mrs. Mary Fletcher*, 97.

62. Mack, *Heart Religion*, 141.

63. Amy Caswell Bratton, *Witnesses of Perfect Love: Narratives of Christian Perfection in Early Methodism* (Toronto: Clements Publishing, 2014), 51.

64. Frank Baker, "John Wesley and Sarah Crosby," *Proceedings of the Wesley Historical Society*, 27, no. 4 (December 1949): 76.

65. Bratton, *Witnesses of Perfect Love*, 51.

66. Leslie Church, *More About Early Methodist People*, rev. ed. (London: Epworth Press, 1955), 149.

67. Bratton, *Witnesses of Perfect Love*, 52.

68. Brown, *Women of Mr. Wesley's Methodism*, 16.

69. Chilcote, ed., *Early Methodist Spirituality*, 81–86.

70. Chilcote, *She Offered Them Christ*, 27.

71. Brown, *Women of Mr. Wesley's Methodism*, 45–46.

72. Quoted in Brown, *Women of Mr. Wesley's Methodism*, 21.

73. Chilcote, *She Offered Them Christ*, 92.

74. Chilcote, *John Wesley and the Women Preachers*, 121.

75. Baker, "John Wesley and Sarah Crosby," 76.

76. Baker, "John Wesley and Sarah Crosby," 76.

77. Zechariah Taft, *Biographical Sketches of the Lives and Public Ministry of Various Holy Women*, Vol. II (London: H. Cullingworth, 1828), 43.

78. Morrow, *Early Methodist Women*, 14.

79. Chilcote, *John Wesley and the Women Preachers*, 121.

80. Chilcote, *Her Own Story*, 80.

81. Chilcote, *John Wesley and the Women Preachers*, 123.

82. Brown, *Women of Mr. Wesley's Methodism*, 26.

83. Chilcote, *John Wesley and the Women Preachers*, 123.

84. Morrow, *Early Methodist Women*, 14.

85. Quoted in Chilcote, *John Wesley and the Women Preachers*, 130.

86. Church, *More About Early Methodist People*, 189.

87. Church, *More About Early Methodist People*, 189.

88. Quoted in Chilcote, *John Wesley and the Women Preachers*, 133.

89. Tolar Burton, *Spiritual Literacy*, 164.

90. Mary Bosanquet Fletcher Letter, Appendix D in Chilcote, *John Wesley and the Women Preachers*, 299.

91. Fletcher Letter, Appendix D in Chilcote, *John Wesley and the Women Preachers*, 300.

92. Fletcher Letter, Appendix D in Chilcote, *John Wesley and the Women Preachers*, 301.

93. Fletcher Letter, Appendix D in Chilcote, *John Wesley and the Women Preachers*, 301.

94. Brown, *Women of Mr. Wesley's Methodism*, 29–30.

95. Chilcote, *John Wesley and the Women Preachers of Early Methodism*, 142.

96. Brown, *Women of Mr. Wesley's Methodism*, 26.

97. Tolar Burton, *Spiritual Literacy*, 164.

98. Fletcher Letter, Appendix D in Chilcote, *John Wesley and the Women Preachers*, 301–302.

99. Fletcher Letter, Appendix D in Chilcote, *John Wesley and the Women Preachers*, 301–302.

100. Fletcher Letter, Appendix D in Chilcote, *John Wesley and the Women Preachers*, 303.

101. Mack and Wilson, "Mary Fletcher's Bible," 62.

102. Mack and Wilson, 'Mary Fletcher's Bible," 303–304.

103. Mack and Wilson, "Mary Fletcher's Bible," 59–61.

104. Chilcote, *John Wesley and the Women Preachers*, 144.

105. Church, *More About Early Methodist People*, 139.

106. Quoted in Chilcote, *John Wesley and the Women Preachers*, 143.

107. Mack and Wilson, "Mary Fletcher's Bible," 62.

108. Gerald R. Cragg, ed. *The Works of John Wesley: Bicentennial Edition*, "The Appeals to Men of Reason and Religion and Certain Related Open Letters," Vol. 11 (Nashville: Abingdon, 1987), 298–299.

109. Chilcote, *John Wesley and the Women Preachers*, 143.

110. Tolar Burton, *Spiritual Literacy*, 163.

111. Quoted in Chilcote, *John Wesley and the Women Preachers*, 144.

112. Telford, ed. *Letters of John Wesley*, accessed March 9, 2020 http: wesley.nnu.edu.john–wesley.the–letters–of–john–wesley.wesleys–letters–1771.

113. Bratton, *Witnesses of Perfect Love*, 55.

114. Morrow, *Early Methodist Women*, 84.

115. Ward and Heitzenrater, eds., *The Works of John Wesley: Bicentennial Edition*, Vol. 22, entry for Sept. 6, 1772, 348.

116. Moore, ed., *Life of Mrs. Mary Fletcher*, 133–5.

117. Moore, ed., *Life of Mrs. Mary Fletcher*, 135–136.

118. Moore, ed., *Life of Mrs. Mary Fletcher*, 137–138.

119. Morrow, *Early Methodist Women*, 86–87.

Chapter Four

1. Moore, ed., *Life of Mrs. Mary Fletcher*, 141.

2. Chilcote, ed., *Early Methodist Spirituality*, 149–150.

3. Paul Chilcote, "An Early Methodist Community of Women," *Methodist History*, 38, no. 4 (July 2000): 226.

4. Mary Bosanquet Fletcher, *Jesus, Altogether Lovely: or a Letter to some of the single women in the Methodist Society*, reproduction from British Library (London: Robert Hawes, 1766), 1–2.

5. Chilcote, "An Early Methodist Community," 226.

6. Fletcher, *Jesus, Altogether Lovely*, 7.

7. Chilcote, "An Early Methodist Community," 228.

8. Fletcher, *Jesus, Altogether Lovely*, 10.

9. Fletcher, *Jesus, Altogether Lovely*, 10.

10. Chilcote, "An Early Methodist Community," 229.

11. Fletcher, *Jesus, Altogether Lovely*, 11.

12. Fletcher, *Jesus, Altogether Lovely*, 12.

13. Chilcote, "An Early Methodist Community," 229.

14. Moore, ed., *Life of Mrs. Mary Fletcher*, 143.

15. Moore, ed., *Life of Mrs. Mary Fletcher*, 153.

16. Morrow, *Early Methodist Women*, 88–89.

17. Morrow, *Early Methodist Women*, 88–89.

18. Janet Burge, *Women Preachers in Community*, Number 12 in series *People Called Methodists* (Peterborough: Foundery Press, 1996), 26.

19. Culley, *British Women's Life Writing*, 42–44.

20. Morrow, *Early Methodist Women*, 91.

21. Quoted in Culley, *British Women's Life Writing*, 34.

22. Quoted in Stanley, *Holy Boldness*, 127.

23. Moore, ed., *Life of Mrs. Mary Fletcher*, 163.

24. Moore, ed., *Life of Mrs. Mary Fletcher*, 163.

25. Telford, ed., *Letters of John Wesley*, http: nnu.edu. john–wesley. the–letters–of–john–wesley. wesleys–letters–1781b, accessed April 25, 2020.

26. Telford, ed., *Letters of John Wesley*, http: nnu.edu. john–wesley. the–letters–of–john–wesley. wesleys–letters–1781b, accessed April 25, 2020.

27. Quoted in Janet Burge, "Impudent Women," *Epworth Review* 21, no. 2, 97.
28. Quoted in Morrow, *Early Methodist Women*, 92.
29. Brown, *Women of Mr. Wesley's Methodism*, 145–146.
30. Tolar Burton, *Spiritual Literacy*, 272–273.
31. Tolar Burton, *Spiritual Literacy*, 170.
32. Moore ed., *Life of Mrs. Mary Fletcher*, 164.
33. Moore, ed., *Life of Mrs. Mary Fletcher*, 176.
34. Church, *More about Early Methodist People*, 141.
35. Lloyd, *Women and the Shaping of British Methodism*, 35.
36. Moore, ed., *Life of Mrs. Mary Fletcher*, 130, 132.
37. Moore, ed., *Life of Mrs. Mary Fletcher*, 191–195.
38. Brown, *Women of Mr. Wesley's Methodism*, 147.
39. Gareth Lloyd, "Repression and Resistance: Wesleyan Female Public Ministry in the Generation after 1791," *Angels and Impudent Women: Women in Methodism* (papers given at the 2005 Conference of The Wesley Historical Society), Norma Virgoe, ed., (Loughborough: Teamprint), 118.
40. Culley, *British Women's Life Writing*, 45.
41. Gareth Lloyd, "Repression and Resistance," 118.
42. Culley, *British Women's Life Writing*, 45–46.
43. Bruge, *Women Preachers*, 30.
44. Moore, ed., *Life of Mrs. Mary Fletcher*, 333.
45. Mack and Wilson, "Mary Fletcher's Bible," 67.
46. Brown, *Women of Mr. Wesley's Methodism*, 148.
47. Moore, ed., *Life of Mrs. Mary Fletcher*, 426–427.
48. Bruge, *Women Preachers in Community*, 28–30.
49. Lloyd, "Repression and Resistance," 118.
50. Mack, *Heart Religion*, 168–9.
51. Burge, *Women Preachers*, 29.
52. Burge, *Women Preachers*, 30.
53. Mack and Wilson, "Mary Fletcher's Bible," 68.
54. Manuscript journal of Mary Tooth, 30 July 1796 (MCA: MAM Fl. 14. 2B), quoted by Gareth Lloyd, "Introduction to Watchwords," *The Asbury Journal* 61, no. 2 (2006).
55. Mack and Wilson, "Mary Fletcher's Bible," 68.
56. Frudd, "Mary Fletcher as a Source," 99.
57. Mack and Wilson, "Mary Fletcher's Bible," 68.
58. Lloyd, "Introduction to Watchwords," 7–11.
59. Mack and Wilson, "Mary Fletcher's Bible," 71.
60. Tolar Burton, *Spiritual Literacy*, 159.
61. Mack and Wilson, "Mary Fletcher's Bible," 70–71.
62. Wallace, ed., *Susanna Wesley: The Complete Writings*, 109.
63. Lloyd, "Repression and Resistance," 120.

64. Mack, *Heart Religion*, 162.

65. Mary Bosanquet Fletcher, "Watchwords: The Names of Christ," *The Asbury Journal* 61. 2:7–11, 31–32.

66. Fletcher, "Watchwords," 31–32.

67. Mack, *Heart Religion*, 215.

68. Fletcher, "Watchwords," 14–15.

69. Fletcher, "Watchwords," 16.

70. Mack, *Heart Religion*, 215.

71. John R. Tyson, ed., *Charles Wesley: A Reader* (New York and Oxford: Oxford University Press, 1989), 106.

72. Mack, *Heart Religion*, 214–215.

73. Tyson, ed., *Charles Wesley: A Reader*, 102.

74. Fletcher, "Watchwords," 26–27.

75. Fletcher, "Watchwords," 26–27.

76. Fletcher, "Watchwords," 88–89.

77. Fletcher, "Watchwords," 88–89.

78. Fletcher, "Watchwords," 88–90.

79. Fletcher, "Watchwords," 88–90.

80. Baker, "John Wesley and Sarah Crosby," 81.

81. Lawrence, *One Family Under God,* 94.

82. Chilcote, *John Wesley and the Women Preachers*, 201.

83. John C. English, "'Dear Sister:' John Wesley and the Women of Early Methodism," *Methodist History* 33, no. 1 (October 1994): 32.

84. Chilcote, *John Wesley and the Women Preachers*, 216, n. 87.

85. Taft, *Holy Women*, Vol. 2, 103–104.

86. Bratton, *Witnesses of Perfect Love*, 62.

87. Brown, *Women of Mr. Wesley's Methodism*, 175.

88. Manuscript letter of Oct. 29, 1801, quoted in Brown, *Women of Mr. Wesley's Methodism*, 175.

89. Bratton, *Witnesses of Perfect Love*, 63.

90. Bratton, *Witnesses of Perfect Love*, 62.

91. Brown, *Women of Mr. Wesley's Methodism*, 175.

92. Baker, "John Wesley and Sarah Crosby," 81.

93. Taft, *Holy Women*, Vol. 2, 24.

94. Taft, *Holy Women*, Vol. 2, 25.

95. Baker, "John Wesley and Sarah Crosby," 82.

96. Chilcote, *Her Own Story*, 85.

97. David Hempton, *Methodism: Empire of the Spirit* (New Haven: Yale University Press, 2005), 143.

98. Chilcote, *Her Own Story*, 85.

99. Morrow, *Early Methodist Women*, 41.

100. Morrow, *Early Methodist Women*, 41–42.

101. Chilcote, *Her Own Story*, 85.

102. Morrow, *Early Methodist Women*, 43.
103. Frances Pawson, "The Experience of Frances Pawson," in Chilcote, *Her Own Story*, 88.
104. Pawson, "The Experience of Frances Pawson," 88.
105. Pawson, "The Experience of Frances Pawson," 90–91.
106. Morrow, *Early Methodist Women*, 49.
107. Pawson, "The Experience of Frances Pawson," 95.
108. Morrow, *Early Methodist Women*, 49–50.
109. Hempton, *Methodism: Empire of the Spirit*, 143.
110. Quoted in Morrow, *Early Methodist Women*, 51–52.
111. Mack, *Heart Religion*, 125.
112. Brown, *Women of Mr. Wesley's Methodism*, 80.
113. Morrow, *Early Methodist Women*, 52–53.
114. Pawson, "The Experience of Frances Pawson," 95.
115. Pawson, "The Experience of Frances Pawson," 96.
116. Morrow, *Early Methodist Women*, 58.
117. Andrew O. Winckles, *Eighteenth-Century Women's Writing and the Methodist Media Revolution* (Liverpool: Liverpool University Press, 2019), 71.
118. Brown, *Women of Mr. Wesley's Methodism*, 84.
119. Brown, *Women of Mr. Wesley's Methodism*, 81–82.
120. Morrow, *Early Methodist Women*, 58.
121. Pawson, "The Experience of Frances Pawson," 101.
122. Joseph Sutcliffe, "The Experience of Frances Pawson," digitized by Emory University, accessed April 22, 2020 at archive.org. details. 29464346.1913. emory.edu. page. n6. mode. 2up.
123. Ann Tripp, letter to Frances Pawson, in Chilcote, ed. *Early Methodist Spirituality*, 295–296.
124. Morrow, *Early Methodist Women*, 63.

Chapter Five

1. Lloyd, "Repression and Resistance," 118.
2. Moore, ed., *Life of Mrs. Mary Fletcher*, 318.
3. Chilcote, ed., *Early Methodist Spirituality*, 283.
4. Chilcote, ed., *Early Methodist Spirituality*, 283.
5. Chilcote, ed., *Early Methodist Spirituality*, 283–284.
6. Moore, ed., *Life of Mrs. Mary Fletcher*, 324.
7. Culley, *British Women's Life Writing*, 34.
8. Culley, *British Women's Life Writing*, 56.
9. Lloyd, "Repression and Resistance," 118.
10. Moore, ed., *Life of Mrs. Mary Fletcher*, 346.
11. Culley, *British Women's Life Writing*, 56.
12. Krueger, *Reader's Repentance*, 43, 61.

13. Lawrence, *One Family Under God*, 150.
14. Moore, ed., *Life of Mrs. Mary Fletcher*, 320–321.
15. Chilcote, ed., *Early Methodist Spirituality*, 326.
16. Chilcote, ed., *Early Methodist Spirituality*, 326.
17. Moore, ed., *Life of Mrs. Mary Fletcher*, 363.
18. Chilcote, ed., *Early Methodist Spirituality*, 330.
19. Moore, ed., *Life of Mrs. Mary Fletcher*, 354–355.
20. Chilcote, ed., *Early Methodist Spirituality*, 330.
21. Moore, ed., *Life of Mrs. Mary Fletcher*, 364–365.
22. Chilcote, ed., *Early Methodist Spirituality*, 323.
23. Culley, *British Women's Life Writing*, 55, 61.
24. Lawrence, *One Family Under God*, 181.
25. Church, *More About the Early Methodist People*, 146.
26. Church, *More About the Early Methodist People*, 163.
27. Chilcote, ed., *Early Methodist Spirituality*, 291–292.
28. Chilcote, ed., *Early Methodist Spirituality*, 293.
29. Chilcote, ed., *Early Methodist Spirituality*, 294.
30. Brown, *Women of Mr. Wesley's Methodism*, 240.
31. Brown, *Women of Mr. Wesley's Methodism*, 16, 23.
32. Chilcote, ed., *Early Methodist Spirituality*, 298.
33. Chilcote, ed., *Early Methodist Spirituality*, 300.
34. David R. Wilson, "Church and Chapel: Methodism as Church Extension," Geordan Hammond and Peter S. Forsaith, eds., *Religion, Gender, and Industry: Exploring Church and Methodism in a Local Setting*, (Eugene, Oregon: Pickwick Publications, 2011), 72.
35. Wilson, "Church and Chapel," 74.
36. Culley, *British Women's Life Writings*, 61.
37. Taft, *Holy Women*, Vol. 2, 229.
38. Culley, *British Women's Life Writings*, 34.
39. Culley, *British Women's Life Writings*, 36.
40. John H. Lenton, "Support Groups for Methodist Women Preachers 1803–1851," *Religion, Gender, and Industry*, Hammond and Forsaith, eds., 142.
41. Carol Blessing, "'O that the Mantle May Rest on Me.'" *Religion, Gender, and Industry*, Hammond and Forsaith, eds., 158–159.
42. Chilcote, ed., *Early Methodist Spirituality*, 335.
43. Chilcote, ed., *Early Methodist Spirituality*, 339.
44. Burge, *Women Preachers in Community*, 31.
45. Jean Miller Schmidt, *Grace Sufficient: A History of Women in American Methodism 1760–1939* (Nashville: Abingdon Press, 1999), 52.

CPSIA information can be obtained
at www.ICGtesting.com
Printed in the USA
BVHW031027120221
599995BV00007B/119